# HOW TO MAKE MONEY IN YOUR SPARE TIME BY WRITING

Edited
*by*
KIRK POLKING

# *THE WRITER'S DIGEST GUIDE*

Galahad Books • New York City

**HOW TO MAKE MONEY IN YOUR SPARE TIME
BY WRITING**

Library of Congress Catalog Card Number : 73-81640
ISBN 0-88365-064-9

Published by arrangement with Cornerstone Library Publications

Manufactured in the United States of America

# Contents

# The Easiest Way to Get Started

## Selling fillers, clippings, and short humor to magazines

*by Evelyn P. Johnson*

SEVERAL YEARS AGO a neighbor asked if she might take a pile of old newspapers I was going to throw in the garbage. When I saw her again she complained, "I couldn't get any sense at all out of those newspapers—you'd chopped 'em so full of holes there was no reading left!"

And indeed I had. What my neighbor didn't know was that every hole I'd cut in the papers was a potential check in my mailbox.

Perhaps some cynical reader thinks I've got holes in my *head.* All right. So how are *you* reading your newspaper? Do you glance at the headlines, read the obits and the comics?

Not too much there, I'll admit, although a fellow-writer did find an idea in the funnies for a quiz which sold to a Sunday school paper for several dollars.

I search diligently through every newspaper for pot-boilers. In case the term is unfamiliar, a pot-boiler is a small item that keeps the writing fever aflame (and the postage fund solvent) between the rejections and checks on larger manuscripts. It may be a short, humorous news item; an unusual personal experience. And it isn't unusual for a pot-boiler to bring a larger check than the manuscript. One clipping netted me a total of $55.00. Others have sold for from $5 to $10, and many more have brought in crisp one-dollar bills.

After I read the headlines and the lead stories, I look for items that are not so prominently played up. At the end of a column on an inside page recently I found a short item about a farmer losing his pecan trees. If the trees had died, or if they had been cut down by vandals, they would not have been fuel for my fire. But these trees were stolen. Bark, roots and branches. Funny, huh? Not to the farmer. But the check that I received from a farm magazine for this clipping made *me* smile—$5 worth. And the same mail brought another payment of $5 for a clipping telling of drunken hogs leading officers to the location of a whiskey still in a southern state.

If I find a story about a new method for growing watermelons, an idea for purchasing a bull for community use, etc., I clip the item, paste it on a full-size sheet of typing paper, together with the dateline and the name of the paper. Then I type my name and address in the upper lefthand corner of the sheet, just as on regular manuscripts, and mail the item to an appropriate farm magazine, enclosing the usual self-addressed, stamped envelope.

At first I was careless about keeping records, thinking it a waste of time. If the clipping sold, I would receive payment; if it didn't I had no further use for it anyway. Experience, that famed teacher, taught me this haphazard method did not pay.

A friend and I had submitted the same clipping once. The editor liked it, but he had lost track of whose clip reached him first. He queried both of us for our records. My friend had a record of the date she sent in her clipping. I didn't. I distinctly remembered sending it, and told him so, but admitted frankly that I did not know when. Nice guy that he is, he split the check, paying me $5 that I really did not deserve. Now, I keep an accurate record of when the clipping goes out and to whom.

A newsbreak is often an error that escaped the proofreader. It should be funny enough to embarrass the editor of the publication in which it appears.

One newsbreak I sold was an announcement of a Christmas party-meeting of a woman's club. The item read, in part, "Bring your husbands and gifts for exchange." Some party that must have been! (I went out on the town with the $5 payment the editor sent me.)

A printer of a large daily garbled two items—one about home permanents and one about food. The result read: "The waving lotion may cause painful irritation if it gets into flavored MF chip dip its delicious." An editor liked this one too.

Some magazines also buy short, pithy sentences clipped

from newspapers. I sold this one from a southern weekly: "When day is done, isn't it disgusting that nothing else is?"

In an ad section of a daily I found this: "Lost, small boy mare." If you know anything at all about animals, you'll recognize a mixture of sexes here which makes the ad humorous.

Some clippings bring two checks. A relative called my attention to an ad in our weekly paper which stated that a comfortable lounge, complete with TV and soft drinks, had been added to a cotton gin for the farmers who had to wait their turn at the gin.

The news clippings sold to *Farm Journal* for $10, and I queried the editor of *Progressive Farmer* in regard to an article. He was interested in seeing a few hundred words on this lounge, and added that he would send a photographer to get pictures. A letter to the owner of the gin, in an adjoining county, brought all the information I needed, with a bit of human interest about a local farmer, and I mailed the manuscript out. The editor paid me $15. That's a cotton pickin' sale. (Ed. Note: This author knew the editors of both these farm publications and was a regular contributor to both so felt she was on ethical ground here—but it is *not* advisable, under normal circumstances, to sell even a filler and then a more complete article on the same subject to two magazines competing in the same field.)

*The Furrow* paid $5 each for clippings about 1) a man who made leather saddles, and 2) a man who gathered herbs and sold them.

*Guideposts* buys a number of short features for its various departments.

Editors don't always include in the information about their needs in market lists that they buy clippings, but as in all phases of writing one learns by trial-and-error. If I find a story which I think might appeal to the editor of a certain publication, I gamble a couple of stamps and mail him the clipping. I have opened up a couple of new markets in this manner, and have been assigned articles in other instances.

Reading separate short items about the high cost of clearing litter from our highways, and how the idleness of youth contributes to delinquency, I came up with a suggestion on organizing Clean-Up Squads among teenagers for cleaning the roadsides. A religious publication for teenagers paid me $5 for this hint.

In a column for young folks I found interesting mention of the common pin, or straight pin. This set me to thinking, and I went to the encyclopedia for more information. Five hundred words on the pin from its first use to the present day sold to a little hardware trade journal, for a cent a word.

In another column, a writer mentioned the parts of the human body in a humorous way that gave me an idea for a quiz. *Grit* bought it for $2.

Curious or odd items gleaned from newspapers have sold to *Grit* for $1 each. Example: A man named Peter Rabbit had a brother named Jack and a sister named Bunny. For this market I never use the clipping itself, but merely type the item, reworded as concisely as possible, onto a postal card. The card is addressed to: "Curiodities, *Grit*, Williamsport, Penn."

I keep a record of the submission, but I do not expect to hear from it unless it is used. And *Grit* does not send tear sheets or complimentary copies.

I have sold *Grit* several rewrites of unusual stories, too, for $1 to $3 each, depending upon the length. I never use an item just as it is, unless submitting it to a market which uses clippings. The reason for rewriting the story is that there are laws against piracy and plagiarism, but none against using and reusing ideas culled from newspapers.

My hometown weekly ran a picture of a local woman wearing a hat she had made from corn husks. I interviewed the woman, found she had made part of her living at this hobby in past years and still worked at it despite her 80 years. An article to *The Furrow*, with a how-to slant and a farm angle, brought $40 and the opportunity of working personally with one of their editors. A different slant, stressing the benefit she derived from the hobby angle, sold to *Mature Years* for $15.

An insurance company in Memphis, Tennessee, ran an ad in the *Commercial Appeal*. In the fine print they asked for jingles playing up their insurance services. I sold them a four-line verse for $2. Other writers in my area said they did not see the advertisement. It may pay to advertise, but it also pays to read the advertisements.

I use scissors and paste in my business of mining newspapers for nuggets of gold. But I have learned that I also must use my head. I never try to sell a syndicated release to a market which buys the actual clipping. All newspapers have access to the wire services, so the chances are great that any editor to whom I might submit such a clipping will see the story long before I could get it to him by mail.

As in regular writing, I always enclose a return, *and stamped,* envelope. UNLESS I am submitting to a market which states no return of material will be made.

I remind myself constantly that the old adage about the early bird applies to writing as well as worm-digging, so I try to keep my submissions current with the news. This does not apply to informative material on various subjects which may be filed for future use.

I bear in mind that a subject which is interesting enough to induce an editor to run a story on it, or a letter-to-the-editor, is interesting enough to develop further. I keep a file of clippings that makes my house a haven for all the neighborhood mice and silverfish. From this file I have written and sold quizzes, short stories, articles for both secular and religious magazines, and even verse.

Some people buy newspapers for reading. I buy them to read, too, but I get my money back—and more—by "chopping 'em full of holes" to get the material I sell to other publications.

# How to Sell Articles without Leaving Home

## When you can't get out to do in-depth interviewing or library research

### by Emalene Shepherd

I AM A LAZY writer who works only two hours a day at home, yet I earn several hundred dollars each year by selling magazine articles. If you, too, have limited time for writing, dislike leg work, shun libraries, and do not have to depend upon writing for your livelihood, you can be a selling writer without leaving home.

As every article writer knows, he must back up his ideas with statistics, quotes, and anecdotes. Writing that is "off the top of his head" will not sell.

Sources of information available to the at-home writer are:

1. *Newspapers.* Never let a day go by without clipping at least one article idea from your paper. For example, one morning I read about a boy who had hurt his leg on a barbed wire fence. He was afraid to let his parents know where he had been, and when his leg became infected, he wore two pair of socks for a few days before they discovered his injury. By then, he had to be hospitalized. On this incident I based an article, "Secrets —Good or Bad?" It was published in the juvenile magazine, *Straight.*

A newspaper story about the origin of names prompted "A Rose by Any Other Name," an article that sold to *American Baby.*

An ad in the classified section furnished the idea for "The Telephone Minister." The word, "Troubled?", followed by a number to dial for help, caught my eye. I called the number, interviewed the kindly voice on the other end of the wire, and sold the resulting article to *Success Unlimited* at 5 cents per word.

Another one I sold to that magazine was suggested by a doctor's column in which he discussed headaches. Since he was a local person, I called him and asked permission to quote some of his material. He not only gave his verbal O.K., but he confirmed it by mail and sent me several pamphlets that he had written on the subject. Again I collected 5 cents a word for "How to Guard Against Headaches."

Newspapers also carry statistics and short factual items. I clip them, staple them to a yellow second-sheet, and file them for future use in a folder beside my typewriter.

2. *Magazines.* Other writers often stir me to action when I disagree with them. Experts have flooded the market with advice to parents on how to give "security" to their children. I was so incensed at one piece by an author who obviously had no children of his own that I wrote, "Children Owe Us Something, Too!", with the theme that parents need their own security boosted once-in-awhile by receiving love and understanding from their offspring. It was published in *The Christian Home.*

Once I was reading an advertisement for a liquid product guaranteed to give one an unforgettable New Year's Eve, when I recalled my own past celebrations. The one that topped all of them was a candlelight service at church. "Start the New Year Right" sold to *Together* magazine.

3. *Relatives.* Conversations with my parents, husband and son furnish endless article ideas. One day my father and I were discussing a fishing trip we had taken when I was ten years old. When our boat almost upset in the middle of Lake Erie, he cautioned me, "Always row *against* the waves; if you go with them, you could capsize." The result. "Row Against the Waves," was published in *Success Unlimited.* I have sold more than thirty articles to that magazine, such as: "Quiet—Hospital Zone," about my father's unhappy experiences with visitors when he was ill, "Down With Togetherness," lamenting the lack of privacy in ranch-style homes, and "It's Great to be 40!", an inspirational piece with the theme that maturity has its rewards.

"The Day I Met My Mother," published in *Companion,* carried the message that one never appreciates his parents to the fullest extent until he himself has a child. I illustrated it with experiences from my childhood and adult years. My mother also set me thinking about the Christmas gift that was most significant to me through the years, a kneeling camel paperweight, and I wrote, "The Precious Camel," deploring breakable plastic toys of the modern day. Another article, "You Must Make a Decision," stemmed from my childhood when I was given only ten cents to spend on a shopping tour. In expanding my theme, I showed how being forced to make a choice in small things can help one to make wise decisions in monumental crises.

My husband, too, likes to reminisce about his youth. When he bragged on his mother's cooking, I wrote, "Hurrah for the Frozen Pumpkin Pie!" It appeared in a Thanksgiving issue of *Christian Herald,* probably because the editor, as I did, gave thanks for modern inventions and had no desire to return to "the good old days."

The editor of a confession magazine bought "A Love Affair With Your Wife," inspired by my husband's bringing me a single rose from the yard before he left for work. I tried to show other men how to make a woman happy with small remembrances. "Let's Put Magic Back Into Christmas," emphasizing the importance of family traditions, also sold to a confession magazine.

If you have children, listen and observe. If not, go where the action is. Religious papers are open markets for material about young people. Some of my sales containing advice aimed at them are: "How To Live With Adults," "Everybody Has Problems," and "How To Let Go of Your Parents." I knew one boy whose parents had split up and he was living with his sister. For him I wrote, "If Your Parents Are Divorced . . ." with the theme that his life need not be shattered by this unhappy event and that he should enter into church activities. It sold to the Baptist publication, *Teens.* (Although there are taboos in writing for religious magazines, they do use articles on alcoholism, divorce, and other "sins" as long as they are not presented in a favorable light.)

The most frequent complaint of teenagers is, "Nobody understands me." I enlarged on that sad statement from a mother's viewpoint, because if anyone is misunderstood, I am, and I sold the article to *Scholastic Roto.*

The magazine supplement of Sunday newspapers is another possible article market, but most of them are pictorial sections with limited space for freelance work. *The Cincinnati Enquirer,* however, has published seven of my humorous articles. I have written about my husband's cook-outs, my son's rock 'n' roll band practice in our rathskeller, my sagging clothesline, young persons I have met in my living room who apparently have no last names, and other topics related to life in Suburbia.

In writing about your family, remember to give your work Universal Appeal by keeping your reader in mind and slanting your material toward helping him to identify with your experiences. He wants to laugh with you more often than he wants to cry; he wants to say, "Gee, that's the way it happened at our house!"

To quote an editor of *Ingenue Magazine,* from a letter she sent me concerning one of my manuscripts:

"The statistics you include are essentially available to any editorial assistant. Your own experiences, however, are unique and valuable. If you would revise your story somewhat so that it would include more detailed information on your own hardships and ultimate success, I think you will find a sympathetic response from the editors of women's magazines."

4. *Friends.* As an article-writer, you must listen more than you talk. Some ideas I picked up from listening to friends were: "How To Enjoy Mondays," "Why Your Wife Works" and "Women Talk Too Much." In trying to console a friend who was despondent over the loss of her husband, I wrote, "Pick Up the Pieces," published in *The Christian Home.*

Editors of confession magazines bought "Because It's Your Second Marriage," in which I gave tips on etiquette for that occasion, "How To Get Along With a Stepchild," "You Can Earn Money at Home," "Make Every Minute Count," and "When You're Afraid." All of these article ideas originated in my living room.

Of course, you need more background information for every article than appears in the finished product. To that end, I have on my bookshelves a number of helpful reference books, magazines and pamphlets.

An issue of *Good Reading* contains my article, "The Importance of Quitting," with the theme that sometimes one must quit what he is doing to move on to higher achievements.

If you are as enthusiastic about writing as I am, you will never quit that occupation. How else could we collect checks and at the same time satisfy our egos by seeing our name in print without ever leaving home?

# Are You a Greeting Card Buyer?

### Then you can sell ideas to greeting card publishers. Here are 13 tips from a greeting card editor.

*by H. Joseph Chadwick*

GREETING CARD COMPANIES pay about $500,000 a year to free-lance writers. The base rates they pay may run all the way from 75¢ a line for general verse material to $50 for a single studio card gag. And for very special ideas and promotions, most companies will pay even higher!

But although this is one of the most lucrative writing markets there is, it is also one of the toughest to sell. As editor of a leading greeting card company, I receive well over 1,000 ideas a week—and buy an average of less then 1 percent of them.

Yet, almost without fail, I'll buy from two to three new writers each month. Writers who have never before sold me an idea, and who in some cases have never before sold anyone else anything either. It's always a thrill to buy that first idea from them!

It's also a thrill to watch other writers constantly improve. And although they haven't yet sold their first idea, you know it will only be a matter of time and work before they do. Unfortunately, many of them give up before they make that first sale.

But not all of them. Thankfully! Because the greeting card companies need new writers. Not only to replace old writers who leave the field, but also for the freshness of ideas that they bring to greeting cards.

It is these new writers—these talented ones—that editors try to encourage to keep writing. But, unfortunately, there isn't always time to do so. And so we lose some of them. Often, I suppose, because they get to feeling as if they're the *only* writers who aren't making it. As if they're all alone!

As a former freelance writer, I know how cold and lonely it can be at your desk or kitchen table, and I wish I could answer every question I get. But an editor's time is seldom his own. There are always submissions to be read, old cards to rewrite and update, new cards to write, product meetings to attend, deadlines to meet. So there is never enough time for all the questions an editor receives.

Hopefully, then, this article will answer some of these questions. Perhaps some of yours. Questions like these:

1. What is the best form to use in submitting ideas?

For general verse material, use a 3x5 or 4x6 card or slip of paper.

For humorous or studio ideas, use a folded slip of paper or a card dummy. (A card dummy is a sheet of paper or heavier material cut and folded to studio or humorous card size. The idea is then laid out on the dummy just as it would be on a published card, including a rough sketch of some type *if* it helps to enhance the idea.) By hiding the punchline until the buildup has been read, this outside/inside type of presentation for humorous and studio gags helps to retain the element of surprise that is often vital to a particular gag.

*Very important:* Regardless of the type of presentation you use, *don't* clutter up the front of your card or dummy form with *routine* information like your name, address, code number, etc. Put *all* of this information on the *back* of the form, just as it would be on a published card. The *front* of the form should contain only the idea itself.

Some of the cards and dummies I receive have so much typing on the front that I have to hunt for the words expressing the idea. And all this extra glump distracts from the idea and causes it to lose some of its effectiveness. Give your ideas a chance. Don't hide them among a pile of other words!

For general verse, put no more than the verse on the front of the card . . . like this:

EASTER GREETINGS
May this Easter Day
Be a day on which you're blessed
With a heart of deep contentment
And a life of happiness.

HAPPY EASTER

For studio or humorous ideas, no more than the following should be on the front of the card (if you use dummies, the first part would be on the outside, and the last part would be on the inside . . . same for folded slips of paper).

HAPPY BIRTHDAY
Now that you're older, remember
that if you *neck, smoke,* and *drink* . . .
men will call you *fast* . . .
. . . just as *fast* as they can
get to *a phone!*

*Everything* else should go on the back . . . it takes a little more time, but it's well worth it. And you can save a lot of time by buying a rubber stamp for your name and address. You can get one for about $3.00. In the time it will save you, you'll be able to write many more ideas. Maybe one of them will be that $50 one you've been waiting for!

2. I'm using card dummies for my humorous and studio ideas, and I'd like to use a rough sketch to illustrate them . . . but I don't know how to sketch. Is there an easy way to learn enough for simple illustrations?

The easiest way is to buy a bunch of cards that have simple characters on them that demonstrate the various basic emotions: anger, shyness, happiness, sadness, exuberance, slyness, etc. Develop a simple variation of one or more of these characters, and learn to draw them in various positions, and with the different facial expressions needed to show the emotions you want to express. Use these same characters on all the ideas you want to illustrate. It's quite effective, easy to learn, and saves much time.

3. I don't sketch at all. Should I give a word picture of what kind of illustration I think the card should have?

*No!*—except when the illustration is *part* of the idea. With this one exception, I can think of no case where the suggested illustration was used in the published card.

If the illustration is an integral part of the idea, then, of course, suggest it. For example, in this studio idea the illustration is needed to understand the gag:

(Illustration showing rest room
door. Footsteps leading to it) . . .
. . . I hate to see you go . . . even
for a minute! *Hurry Back!*

In the following studio idea, the illustration is not a part of the gag and so it isn't necessary to give a word picture of any type.

To a *Special Guy*
on *Valentine's Day*
If you're thinkin' all you
have to do to get me to kiss
you is pucker up . . .
. . . you're thinkin' right!
HAPPY VALENTINE'S DAY

Giving a word picture when one isn't needed just clutters up your card, distracts from the idea itself, and wastes time that you could be using to develop more ideas.

4. I've made up a list of about 20 greeting card companies from *Writer's Digest, Writer's Market,* and other sources. I plan on sending my ideas to the highest paying markets first, then if they don't sell, to each company down my list. But what do I do with the idea if no one buys it?

Put the idea away in your file, and then about a year from the date you sent it to the first company on your list, start it circulating again. You may even find before you start recirculating it that you can now see how to improve it, because you will obviously improve yourself each year.

But above all, *never, never give up on any idea as long as you believe it is a good idea!* I have sold an idea on its 28th submission. And another writer I know sold an idea five years and 48 submissions after he wrote it, to a company he had submitted it to three times before!

This type of thing happens in all forms of writing, but especially in greeting cards. Editors change for one thing. But more importantly, sentiment and humor are constantly changing things. What was tearfully sentimental twenty years ago is corny today . . . and what is only mildly funny today may be hilarious next year. The same sentiment and humor are still in the idea, but our tastes change. In addition, your ideas may only have been rejected because the editor has no place in his current line to put them even though they may have been perfectly usable ideas. For example, I may have a requirement for only *one* birthday card for a bowler . . . I might buy *one extra* bowler gag for my idea bank (reserve of ideas for future use), but after that I have to turn birthday bowler gags down no matter how good they are.

So keep good ideas going, updating and revising them when you can . . . and *never* give up a *good* idea. It may sell on its next time out!

5. I have a list of greeting card companies, but I don't have the names of all the editors. Is it all right to send my material directly to the company?

No! If you don't know the editor's name, send your material to the type of editor for whom it's intended: General Verse Editor, Humor Editor, Studio Editor, in this manner:

> Studio Editor
> Barker Greeting Card Co.
> 31st and Robertson Sts.
> Cincinnati, Ohio 45209

If you don't address the editor, then the company mail room must open your envelope to find out what's inside and where it goes. This increases the possibility of some of your ideas being lost, or even being damaged by the electric cutters most companies use to open envelopes. It also puts added expense on the company. So always put a *complete address* in your envelope.

6. I have been told that I should use a code number on the back of each of my ideas. What is the best code system to use?

There are more code systems in the greeting card field than there are secret agents on television. Many full-time writers use an elaborate coding system for filing purposes, but for part-time and beginning writers, my personal feeling is that a simple numerical code is best . . . again, to save time. The simplest numerical system possible, of course, is to start numbering your ideas at 1, or 101, or 1001, whichever you prefer, and then continue in sequence. Some writers prefix the number with one or more letters that stand for the type of idea it is—for example: B for Birthdays, GW for Get Wells, etc.

Regardless of what system you use, don't number every idea you write, since you will be writing many more ideas than you will actually be submitting. Only number your ideas when you have them ready for submission. And don't forget to put the same code number on your file copy.

7. What is the simplest way to keep track of where your ideas have been?

For each idea you submit, make up a 3x5 file card. Put the code number of the idea on the front of the card along with the idea itself. On the back of the card, record where you're sending the idea. The simpler the method of recording, the better . . . again, to save time. So always abbreviate the name of the company. For example: H—Hallmark, B—Barker, A—American, RC—Rust Craft, and so on down your submission list.

The first item on the back of your card should include the company, the month, and the year. Like this: B—9/65. This means the idea went first to Barker in September of 1965. The next time it goes out, simply put the company down if it is still the same month. If it is the next month, put down both the company and the month. Don't put down the year until the year changes. If some editor holds the idea or comments on it, note this next to the company when the idea comes back. When you sell the idea, record the actual date of sale, and the purchase price. So a short record on the back of your card might look like this:

        B—9/65
        RC—Held 9-20-65 Ret. 10-11-65
        A10
        BC11—Liked idea, no place for it.
        RS
        OZ12
        V—1/66 Sold 1-14-66 $10.00

When the idea is sold, put the file card into a *sold* file, either under the company it was sold to, or perhaps better still, under the type of card it is: Friendship, Get Well, Christmas, etc. As you sell more and more ideas, these categories can be broken down even further. Such as Get Well/Female, Get Well/Male, Get Well/Hospital, Christmas/General, Christmas/Wife, and so on. So eventually your *sold* file can serve as a handy reference file for generating new ideas in any particular category.

To keep track of ideas that are out, put the file cards of the ideas you are submitting to a particular company together. Then type the name of the company, the number of ideas in the batch, and the date the batch was sent out on another 3x5 card. Secure this cover card to the file cards and file them under a general title of *Submitted.*

8. I submitted some ideas to an editor almost two months ago and haven't heard anything yet. What should I do?

Send a polite query to the editor, enclosing a stamped, self-addressed envelope, asking him to check on the status of your material. This will ordinarily bring a prompt reply. If you still do not hear within two weeks, send another query. If you still do not get an answer, and, unfortunately, this sometimes happens, send a letter stating that if you don't hear anything within 10 days, your ideas (list them) are no longer for sale to that company.

Some writers always register this type of letter and request a return receipt. In any case, always keep a copy of your letter and of the ideas you had submitted for future reference.

If you haven't received an answer by the end of two weeks (always allow a couple of extra days for good measure), make up new roughs and start submitting the ideas to other companies. I'd also suggest you scratch that particular company off of your submission list!

9. I submitted fourteen ideas to a company, and eleven came back with a rejection slip and no mention of the other three ideas. Does this mean they're holding my ideas?

It's possible. There are a couple of editors who hold ideas out of a batch without mentioning it. (That's why you should always count the number of ideas in any returning batch—immediately—before they have a chance to get mixed up with anything else.) Sometime later you either receive your ideas back, or the editor sends you a letter/invoice telling you he is buying your ideas. You simply sign the invoice that is on the bottom of the letter and return it to him. Soon after, you receive your check in the mail. (Speaking of checks, if you don't receive your check within thirty days after an editor tells you he is buying something, or you return his invoice, send a polite query about it.)

It is also possible, of course, that your ideas have been lost or misplaced. So if ideas are missing from your batch, and you don't hear anything about them within from four to six weeks, a polite query is certainly in order.

Under any condition, the best rule to follow with editors is when you are in doubt about something—ask! Time permitting, you will usually get an answer of some sort. And if an editor answers and says he doesn't have your ideas, don't argue with him. He has no reason to lie to you. Simply make up new roughs and start submitting them again.

10. Although it hasn't happened to me yet, I've been very concerned about what I should do if I sell an idea and then soon after spot an identical idea on the market. This must sometimes happen with all the ideas that are being written. What should I do if this happens?

The best thing to do is to write the editor who bought your idea and tell him exactly what happened. If you have not yet been paid for your idea, he will simply stop payment. Or if the check is on the way to you, return it when you receive it. If you've already received the check and cashed it, the simplest thing, from a bookkeeping standpoint, is for you to simply replace the idea with the next one the editor picks to buy. And this is usually what is done. The editor discards, or returns, the identical idea, and then gets a "free" one from you . . . his choice, of course. If some time has passed and your idea has been published before you spot the identical card, then there is obviously nothing that can be done about it, but it's another reason for studying the markets constantly.

Remember, part of an editor's job is to constantly study cards on the market, and it sometimes happens that *he* spots a card that he has just purchased from a writer. This duplication can happen through pure accident, of course—but if it happens too often, the editor becomes somewhat leery of that particular writer's work.

11. I received a market letter from an editor in which he asked for *Everyday* ideas. What are these?

*Everyday* ideas are those ideas that people send *everyday* of the year, as opposed to *Seasonal* ideas that they send only at certain times of the year, such as Christmas. Everyday ideas include Birthdays, Get Wells, Anniversaries, and Friendship cards. Among the Friendship cards may be such special captions as Trip, Vacation, Congratulations, Thank You, New Home, etc.

By the by, when writing ideas, remember that Everyday

ideas make up more than 50 percent of most companies' total output, so spend most of your time on Everyday ideas. Also, out of the Everydays, Birthdays make up more than 50 percent of the line. So concentrate most of your efforts on Birthdays.

12. I don't seem to be able to get enough ideas for, greeting cards—is there any system for generating ideas?

Yes, there are many systems. The two most popular ones are the *Switching* method and the *Association* method.

In the first method, you immerse yourself in greeting cards, kick around the verse or gag, try to see it from a different angle, rewrite it, try to go it one better. Notice I said *rewrite* it—*not* copy it! The rewriting is done by retaining the essence of the idea and building a new verse or gag around it. That this is done constantly can be easily seen by the number of similar (not identical!) cards on the market, and the number of cards playing on the same words or phrase.

For example, these are allowable rewrites of the same basic studio gags, all playing on a phrase from a cigarette commercial (incidentally, TV commercials are an excellent source of material, especially when they use a catch-phrase over and over:

> You're absolutely the greatest, the most satisfying, the least irritating, the coolest . . . in fact . . .
> . . . I'd rather fight than switch!

> I think I know how old you really are . . . but I'd rather fight than snitch!

> Us greeting card senders would rather fight . . .
> . . . than send a present!

All three of these cards are presently on the market, and are high on the best-seller list of the company that published them!

Remember, though, you *cannot* use the same words or phrases that someone else has written—tain't ethical—you can only use the essence of the idea. Study the cards on the stands to see how this is done. Note the number of Get Well studio cards that play a gag around a thermometer or a hypodermic needle. The number of birthday gags based on candles. The number of vacation gags based on spending money. The number of general verse Christmas cards that center around the Holy Family, or the Three Wise Men. And there are undoubtedly thousands of unwritten gags and verses using these same basic ideas that still remain to be written. Perhaps by you!

The second method of generating ideas, and the one that will probably generate the most ideas for you, is the association method.

In this method, you write down a list of things associated with the type of card you are trying to write. For example, if you are writing Father's Day cards, your list will probably contain things like: present, kind of father, kind of day, kids, wish, Sunday, do-it-yourselfer, golfer, fisherman, bowler, sportsman, and as many more as you can think of. By the by, always write your list out new each time. It will help you to get started putting something down on paper, and you might always come up with that new item that will give you an original and fresh approach to your subject.

Once you have your list, let your imagination run free, bounce the items around in your mind, look at them from every possible direction, think of your Uncle George, or your brother Pete, what would you like to say to them? . . . think of your own father, what would you want to say to him on Father's Day? . . . what kind of a father is he? That's it! Take that one item, *kind of a father*, and make up a list of characteristics of a father: kind, thoughtful, patient, generous, wonderful, wise, strong, understanding, etc. . . .

Takes a lot to be a father, doesn't it? Is there an idea there? Let's look at that thought backwards . . . maybe like this:

> It doesn't take much to be a father like you . . .
> . . . just wisdom, patience, kindness, and love!

Not bad for a beginning!

Now let's try a fast list for birthdays. There are lots of things here: gifts, age, money, card, drinking, candles, cake, friends, celebration, and many others. Out of this list, one of the often done studio gags is one based on the card itself—for example, exaggerating how much trouble it was to get the birthday card . . . maybe something like this:

> You won't believe what I went through to get you this birthday card . . .
> . . . my lunch money!

And I bet *you* can think of a lot more and funnier punch-lines than that one! Try it—it's good practice!

And while we're still on the subject of getting ideas, this is a good place to point out the fact that a verse you wrote originally for Father's Day might also be used for a Birthday card. Of course, you can't sell it both ways. But the point is that you can often switch captions on your ideas to fill market requirements.

So if you get a market letter calling for Seasonal cards, look over your Everyday card ideas and see what you can switch the caption or a word or two on and make into a seasonal idea.

13. Now that I'm writing ideas and submitting them, how many should I keep in the mail?

As many as possible! But if you want a goal to shoot for, working part-time you should try to keep a minimum of 500 ideas in the mail. Working full time, 1,000 ideas would be a bare minimum. One of the country's leading greeting card writers keeps between three and four thousand ideas in the mail! How does he do it? Well, I'll have to admit that he has a secret!

He keeps writing!

Cards mentioned in this Chapter through the courtesy of the Barker Greeting Card Co.

# Here are 3 sample "roughs" of card ideas as might be submitted by a freelancer:

## 1.

Happy Birthday ..

Now that you're OLDER .. remember that if you WALK, RUNCH, and DRIVE .. one still will you FAST ...

... just so fast as they can get to a phone!

| NAME | ADDRESS | SONS |
|------|---------|------|

## 2.

I THINK I KNOW HOW OLD YOU REALLY ARE!

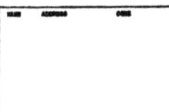

... but I'd rather fight than switch!

Happy Birthday

## 3.

FOR YOUR BIRTHDAY ..
I'D LIKE TO SEND YOU
A TOUCHING LITTLE
SOMETHING TO HELP YOU
REMEMBER THE MANY
QUIET, SENTIMENTAL,
INSPIRATIONAL TIMES
WE'VE SHARED TOGETHER...

(beer bottle cap attachment)

Happy Birthday

# A Seven Letter Word for Money: Puzzles

### How to create them and sell them to magazines

*by Jean Davison*

**D**URING THE PAST nine months I have earned over $500 from crossword puzzles I made in my spare time, but if you want to know a 3-letter word for "Babylonian war god," don't ask *me*—I haven't the foggiest. Which only proves that if you're a typical writer type, one who loves the English language but hates obscure terms, you too may be able to beef up your freelance income by making and selling crosswords.

The easiest way to find out whether puzzlemaking is your cup of Lipton's is to try it.

If you have a crossword puzzle magazine handy, look in the Easy section for a fresh diagram which calls for a 3-letter word at 1-Across and another 3-letter word at 1-Down. Start by filling in the 1-Across space with any common word that begins and ends with a consonant. Next choose any 3-letter word which begins and ends with a vowel and write it directly under the first word.

Obviously not every combination you might come up with will work. For instance, here are two words that don't make the grade:

If you try to continue this crossword by filling in letters that will make words in the Down column, beginning with 2-Down, you'll soon see the problem. APE and APT are the only common 3-letter words which begin with AP. APE is ruled out immediately because crossword editors forbid the use of the same word more than once in a single puzzle, and you've already used APE in an Across position.

APT is unsatisfactory for a different reason.

When you try to fill in 13-Across, you'll discover that there are very few words which have the letter T as their second letter. In fact, the only possibilities begin either with an S (like STAMP or STREAM) or with a vowel (like OTTERS or AT-TICS). None of these words will do because there is no common 3-letter word beginning with CA (1-Down) which *ends* in S or a vowel. (You *could* use the abbreviation CAA at 1-Down, but many editors scowl at abbreviations and exotic words, especially in the small easy puzzles you will probably be submitting to them as your first effort.)

So heave a sigh, erase APE, and try another word. For instance:

This one is duck soup. Begin by filling in 2-Down with the obvious choice, AGE.

For 1-Down there are eight candidates: CAD, CAL, CAM, CAN, CAP, CAR, CAT, and CAW. Pick one at random and continue constructing your first crossword puzzle.

If you reach a point where no word seems to work, backtrack by erasing. Don't lose heart. The more you practice, the easier it gets. Once you get the hang of it, you'll probably find that making puzzles is more diverting, more challenging, and certainly more rewarding moneywise than solving them ever was.

Just a few more tips that should help you start to sell:

1. An unabridged dictionary isn't necessary, but you should have a good current desk-sized edition. (I use the college edition of *Webster's New World Dictionary*.)

2. A crossword puzzle dictionary, available at any newsstand or bookstore, is a valuable aid. Buy one which will give you long lists of 2-, 3-, and 4-letter words arranged alphabetically.

3. You may use the diagrams in any newspaper or crossword magazine as a framework for your own puzzles. Diagram patterns are used over and over; only the arrangement of words within them can be copyrighted.

4. Before submitting puzzles to a magazine, write the editor. Enclose a stamped self-addressed envelope, and request a list of his requirements. Each publisher has his own set of do's and don'ts? Knowing them beforehand will save you a lot of rewriting.

5. Don't overlook any potential markets. Besides the puzzle magazines, there are many other prospective buyers for simple puzzles, such as your local newspaper, juvenile magazines, and various periodicals which use fillers. Other markets, such as trade journals and movie magazines, sometimes take specialty puzzles which contain words relating to their particular fields.

## MORE TIPS FROM A PUZZLE SPECIALIST

For those who would care to try their wits at the construction of interesting 'Topical' cross words, here are some suggestions:

Select a topic covered by a group of magazines, such as sports. Golf, turf and tennis are good subjects and there is little competition in this field.

From authentic sources collect words for a 'word bank' which are pertinent to the subject chosen. Also, make sure you are able to give an accurate and interesting definition of each word gathered.

Place the words in the columns—three letter words in three-letter columns, four-letter words in four-letter columns, etc. . .

This makes the task of finding a six letter word, with the fourth letter required to be a particular letter easier to find. Just glance down your six-letter columns until you locate the first that meets the requirements. It is much easier than trying to think of a word the fourth letter of which is such and such.

In the event you do not have a word in your word bank that will fit, then it is necessary to refer to the dictionary and use a non-topical word. But keep these to a minimum.

Once you have collected as large a word bank as you are able, (and the larger your word bank, the easier it is to construct a puzzle) you are ready to commence construction.

Diagrams must be symmetrical and can not have dangling letters, nor too many black squares.

The diagram is a very important part of the puzzle, as the constructor grows more proficient he may use more difficult diagrams, but at first he should not attempt these. When several lengthy words run alongside of each other, either horizontally or vertically, it makes the fitting in of words much more difficult, and many times impossible.

In double spaced typing follow the form below:

### HORIZONTAL

| Zebra | 1. | Convict horse. |
| Cow | 4. | Bovine |

After typing the horizontal list, continue with the vertical. The column on the left is for the editor to check by if he cares to do so. The numbers and definitions to the right of the number are all that will be printed.

Numbering the diagram is simple. Each white box is numbered in consecutive order, beginning with the number one, and reading left to right, horizontally across the page.

These numbers are to be typed in at the top left corner of each box. Two india ink camera-ready drawings are made. One with the numbers only, the other without the numbers but with the letters of the solution neatly lettered in the proper spaces. I use a lettering guide to do this and the drawings come out very well.

Puzzles are commonly made in sizes of thirteen by thirteen, or fifteen by fifteen; that is, the same number of boxes horizontally as vertically.

Before the puzzle is submitted for publication, check everything for accuracy—drawings, numbering and spelling.

*—Harry R. Feuersinger*

# Beginning Writer's Bonanza

### 2,000 Trade Journals
*Have you an idea to sell them? Here's how to get started*

*by Robert Hays*

WRITERS COME IN three models—the often published, the sometimes published, and the never published. If you belong to the first group, go back to your typewriter while the rest of us talk about part-time freelancing—how to net more (second group) or get published (third group).

Part-time writing is no smooth interstate highway to riches. But in bumping along the cobblestones of part-timing, you can (1) make the most of your limited time (2) sell more and (3) net more from the articles you sell. How?

*Step One:* Work for a writer's only credentials—bylines and checks, not rejection slips. Look for the paying market. You'll almost certainly get more bylines and checks for nonfiction, especially for trade journal articles.

Study yourself, your background, and your situation. Which fields do you already know? Where can you dig under the surface for more than a newspaper reporter's treatment of a story?

(1) Pick subjects where you know the major problems, and preferably some answers. An outsider might think that *Gas* magazine wants articles about cooking ranges. But a kitchen range has usually much less of a "load" than a water heater or a central furnace. So unless you can find a story about how Joe Smoe Gas Company doubled its sales of ranges, you're probably wasting your time getting the facts about sales of ranges. If you want to write for gas magazines, you should know this type of fact.

(2) Pick subjects where you speak your reader's language. In writing for petroleum magazines like *Gas* or *Butane-Propane*

*News*, you should know to forget the metric system. Your readers, (so far, at this time of writing) measure heat in BTU (or therms), weight in pounds, temperature in Fahrenheit degrees, etc.

(3) Pick subjects where your regular job can help. I teach in a technical school, so naturally began by writing for the technical trade journals. (If you're a housewife, you deal regularly with retail merchants who are also sources of trade journal articles—Ed.)

Almost anyone can find a market among the hundreds of trade journals listed in the latest *Writer's Market*, an annual directory of free lance markets. Some buy only from assigned writers and staffers. A few pad with press hand-outs. Even so, the trade journals probably average six outside articles each month—a total monthly potential for you of probably five thousand openings.

On your regular job, you probably read several trade journals in your field. For example, the 1971 *Writer's Market* currently shows

7 in insurance

27 in banking and business

58 in education

and even seven for hardware stores and locksmiths. So try to write for the market you already know. If you know your subject, editors will listen to you.

In selling to trade journals you should gross between $75 and $150 per article. When you develop skill in handling a trade journal assignment, you can net from $10 to $15 per hour for your effort.

If you lack courage to try the trade journals, start with the house organs—perhaps your own organization's house organ first. Some house organs pay only in free copies. But you almost always get that byline. Later, when you query a paying editor, you can mention your previous publications. Even if he knows your previous "sales" have paid only in credit-lines, he will still respect you for working at your profession.

Editors really do look for working writers—especially in the lesser known magazines like trade journals. Francis Smith, retired editor of *Southern Engineering*, used to issue a letter asking for articles from industrial people about their jobs. But Francis once told me: "I always ask would-be writers: 'What have you written?' Too often they answer 'Not anything, but I want to be a writer'."

*Step Two:* Look for ideas for assignments. You must learn what an editor wants—advice repeated many times but often ignored.

In trade journals, for example, an editor wants a story about making more money, cutting costs, or improving operations. The subject should be new enough to be worth reading about, but still commercially feasible. A story about irrigating the Mohave Desert by siphoning water across the mountains from the Pacific sounds fascinating. Unfortunately, the idea won't work.

*Step Three:* Ask an editor for an assignment. Most magazine editors prefer queries. You should too. An answered query at least tells you when you are wasting your time. Your query should have four parts:

(1) Start with a snappy lead—a "hook"—which may later become your lead in your article.

(2) Sink the hook—give the editor a few highlights of your story. If you have a plant engineering story, tell him how many man-hours the PERT system saved or how numerically controlled tooling cut maintenance.

(3) Show your qualifications. If you have never written for this editor before, convince him you can do a good research and writing job.

(4) Ask for an assignment.

Suppose you have just learned about a beer plant that uses lots of natural gas in brewing. So you write the editor of a magazine which publishes for the gas industry. Here is the first paragraph of a sample query (with the name of the company deleted, because I am still working on the assignment):

> Dear Editor:
> XYZ Brewing Company, of Anytown, uses 16,300,000 pounds of grits, 391,000 pounds of hops and water from two 1,200 foot wells each year. But the unsung ingredient in this company's annual beer production, is the fact that the entire brewery operates on natural gas.

Next you should offer perhaps two paragraphs of specifics —the highlights—about the story. Select facts which best fit the magazine's readership. Then, cite a couple of recent publications, or state your experience in the field. And finally, ask for an assignment.

While you wait for an answer, look for other assignments. If one editor says "no" to your query, you will have either another market to try it with or another idea ready for a different magazine. *Never* stop with one writing idea.

If you have never worked for this editor, he will probably invite you to submit the article "on speculation." He can still reject your completed article, but at least he is interested.

You will find most editors nice people. *Writer's Digest* occasionally prints "Storm Warnings" about editors who mistreat writers (by not paying, not answering, etc.). But only one editor ever "beat" me, and only one chiseled a story idea—a small percentage.

*Step Four:* When your answer comes, get busy on the story!

You can make or break yourself in actually doing the story, especially if you must travel. Unlike the full-time pros, you must schedule your research outside your regular job. If your job really prevents you from traveling, you can write articles only about your company, your area, or your industry. Or you can try poetry or fiction.

But you can probably squeeze some research into a schedule. You can use Saturdays for article research. Many business houses and nearly all travel resorts stay open on Saturday.

You can write on your vacation too. One summer I lectured on part-time freelancing at the annual Institute in Technical and Industrial Communications in Colorado. Along the way I picked up three trade journal articles for sure, plus a good chance at a travel article.

Plan your travel carefully—before you leave. Get definite appointments with anybody you must interview. Check Dun and Bradstreet's *Million Dollar Directory* for the names of businesses in the cities you will visit.

Try for several stories in the same area. You can't "cover the waterfront." But do broaden your background into two or three related areas to get the most research mileage. For example, I did an article about one of the Jacksonville, Florida gas dealers. But I found another story on the same trip. One dealer sent his company car to pick me up at a competitor's office.

In making money writing, you must watch your net. As a part-timer, you will seldom travel on chubby expense accounts. So:

(1) Stay in commercial hotels. You won't have time to

swim in a motel pool anyway. You can get a good room at commercial rates for $8 to $12 a day.

(2) Travel tourist class if you have to fly. Buy your champagne on the ground after your royalty check comes.

(3) Use night letters instead of full-rate telegrams. Night letters attract just as much attention and give you many more words for the money.

(4) Watch for spin-off stories. I once did an article on a gas dealer's tank-unloading methods. The same dealer turned out to have a first-rate story on gas carburetion as well.

(5) Keep track of expenses. You can deduct most of them on your tax return.

(6) If you are really short on expense money, ride a bus.

(7) When you return, check the smaller, off-brand car-rental companies for cars to be returned. They may let you return a car for a much-reduced rate. (Some, however, have cars moving so many places, you can't get a price advantage there on a one-way return.)

(8) Use oil-company credit cards to work on someone else's money without interest, until your check comes in.

(9) If you need a shower and shave before an appointment, offer the desk-clerk of a commercial hotel or motel $2 to let you use a room which he has not cleaned up. (He will furnish towels and soap.) Some cafés catering to truck drivers have public showers; also many state and national parks (although these are outside or between towns).

(10) In researching during the family vacation, consider travel trailering. Pulling a trailer will probably add about one cent a mile to your gasoline costs. But you can cut both motel bills and food bills. One summer, I took my wife and three kids 6,600 miles by travel trailer. Our trailer parking cost us from nothing (in some public parks), to $4.00 (near Disneyland). My family will spend at least $12 a day in restaurants. In a travel trailer we can eat for little more than we spend at home.

(11) Above all, stay alert for ideas. At one writer's conference would-be writers fretted over the lack of article ideas. Less than a block away was a very fine college bookstore. So I broke my own rule of *don't write anything unless you have an assignment.* With a free two hours, I gambled on getting an assignment. I got the facts and sold the story to *College Store.*

*Step Five:* Work at writing professionally. A young friend of mine knows that poetry will not pay for a Cadillac. But—he hasn't written even a line of poetry in months. He should *get to work.*

Develop all the skills you need and buy the equipment for your trade. For example, photography is vital in most nonfiction writing. Press handout pix often do not show what you want, and a pro photographer will charge too much (remember the net!)

I use two single-lens Yashica Pentamatics. But buy and learn to use equipment. And take plenty of pictures—supplies are cheap, and you can't go back for retakes.

It may pay you to develop skill in drafting and using lettering sets (LeRoy, Doric, etc.). Slide-rule proficiency may also help you.

You probably already know how to type. You can save expenses at first by typing your own manuscripts. As you build up assignments, you can hire out the typing—to leave your free time for writing.

Keep books carefully. You must pay tax on your income. With careful bookkeeping you can deduct travel expenses, depreciation, and repairs. Investigate the tax shelter and deductions for part of your home expenses (see *Writer's Digest* April, 1970). You do not have to make money or write as a career, but you must be able to prove to the government that you are *trying* to make money writing. Each year buy the paperback booklet *Your Federal Income Tax* from the Superintendent of Documents.

Build your own library. Because of the articles I specialize in, I find the following books very useful: *The World Almanac* (every year); a dictionary, of course; Roget's Thesaurus; a dictionary of science and a dictionary of business; and a technical handbook.

If you write part time, you are your own worst enemy. If you have a regular paycheck coming in, you will be tempted to postpone your writing. If you're a wife and mother, you'll find your creative juices called on a hundred other ways every day. Even with a definite assignment from an editor—you will find television alluring, that book you haven't read doubly seductive, a ready alibi in your weariness from the day's work. Maybe it's fortunate that so many people want to be writers but so few want to write. But to make anything as a part-timer, you must go about it as a business. You must work.

# How to Sell a Nonfiction Book Idea

### Whether it's a cookbook, a handicraft manual or how to catch a husband in 10 easy lessons.

*by Ross R. Olney*

P UT YOURSELF IN the book editor's chair for a moment. Every day he faces book manuscripts he didn't ask for, nonfiction queries which run to as many pages as a few of today's best sellers, and confusing queries from unknown writers about subjects for which he has no enthusiasm.

No wonder he assigns so few books. Why should he send a contract, and an advance, on an idea he can't understand from a person he doesn't know?

Let's face it . . . he wouldn't be an editor long if he did. Then he would have to go back to freelancing, and where does that leave all of us freelancers? The field is crowded enough as it is.

"But I don't know any book editor personally," you say, "and my idea is *not* readily understood or appreciated."

Join the club. That was my position, and still is. Yet I've pulled in several hard cover contracts in the past year, and expect to pull in more this year.

How did I do this? I try to write the original query from the editor's point of view. I try to make him happy, make him know me, fire him up with my idea . . . and I don't take all day about it.

I do this with three separate pages, single spaced . . . neatly!

Since I am not a well-known writer, I save the introduction page until last, at first trying to put across my idea and my way of handling it.

Let's pick a book subject. How about *Daredevil of the Speedways?* That's a straightforward idea for a nonfiction book. First, on page one of the three pages, sell the idea. Consider this page a magnificently short article on the subject, written directly to the editor.

You might start with "There is a sport in the United States in which few people will ever participate, but in which they all have some degree of interest." Or, "Ascot, Langhorne, Phoenix . . . Indianapolis, names which send a chill, or a thrill, through the heart." Or, "Not ONE hard cover book has ever been published on the champions of big time auto racing, yet this sport outdraws ALL others in attendance." Regarding the last one, editors enjoy the idea, or the dream, of selling thousands of books. Give it the old hard sell, by all means.

Fill page one, single spaced, with your marvelous subject. Add facts, figures, and anecdotes to prove your point. Wrap it up with a projected book length, and whatever photo possibilities this subject might have, if it has any. Most likely the editor will change the length, but that doesn't matter at this point.

Page two of your query is a chapter breakdown. Say "Chapter One" and follow this, briefly, with what you intend to say in chapter one. Then, "Chapter Two", and so on. This convinces the editor that you know what a book looks like. Be sure to include the most fascinating facts at your disposal (even though the editor will realize that, at this point, you have not yet started *concentrated* research).

Page three is your own public relations plug area. Drag up from your past every possible reason why you, and nobody else, should be writing this book. Mention your other credits, if you have any. Mention how long you have been writing. *Writing*, not necessarily selling. You don't have to lie if you just say the good things, and you shouldn't lie. You'll be surprised at how good you look if you only consider the happy side.

That's all there is to it. No query is fool-proof, I suppose, but this form has worked for me with editors who are complete strangers to me and my previous work. They seemed to appreciate the informational brevity of it. Give it a try. It can't cost you more than a little time and three sheets of paper . . . and you might find a contract in the return mail for your book idea. I did. My *Daredevil of the Speedways* was bought and published by Grosset and Dunlap!

# How to Become a Newspaper "Stringer"

### If you live near a medium-sized city, there's an opportunity for you to earn while you learn

*by Irene Sullivan*

I F YOU LIVE *near* a city the size of Pomona, Calif.; Orlando, Fla.; Bridgeport, Conn.; Peoria, Ill., or Amarillo, Texas— a city with a population between 50,000 and 150,000—you may be able to land a part-time job that (1) pays well and steadily, (2) isn't time-consuming, (3) offers valuable writing experience, and (4) is personally satisfying.

For in cities of this size, cities which have a medium-size daily newspaper, there's one person who needs you. He's the state editor on that daily newspaper. To get you, he will usually offer a package of benefits: money, time, variety and convenience. Best of all, the job requires only an hour or two daily —more if you wish—and can be done largely from your telephone.

The plain, hard fact is that state editors across the country desperately need correspondents who are also good writers and reporters. While the larger newspapers can afford to dispatch reporters to outlying circulation areas, and small newspapers depend almost entirely on the wire services and local news, the medium-size newspaper is different. It doesn't have a large budget, but neither does it have the limitations of the small newspapers. To get the news from its trade area, it cultivates correspondents working out of the state desk. For example, our paper has a circulation of about 30,000 and we have 15 correspondents from 12 to 60 miles away.

Newspaper corresponding can be both financially and psychological satisfying, yet it is often overlooked by freelancers.

A discouraged young man who gave up freelancing for full-time newspaper work and recently took over the state desk of a Midwestern daily said: "If I'd known then what I know now —how desperate editors really are for good copy—I wouldn't be here now." That's how lucrative corresponding can be.

## A Correspondent's Duties

Each day, either over the phone, through the mails or via the bus lines, the state editor and his correspondents keep in touch. Occasionally the editor wants specific news from his correspondents, such as reports of a statewide referendum for farmers or Jaycees. More often, the correspondent is expected to regularly tap his own news sources and report what he has found. Because news depends on immediacy, and we are an evening paper, we often take important items over the phone from our correspondents right after they break. For example, last week we had some damaging wind and rain in our area, so we had our correspondents phone in any damage reports. If a jury reaches a verdict in time for our state editions, our correspondents phone this news in also. In other words, any news that's important enough and would suffer by being kept overnight is phoned in. We have a WATS (Wide Area Telephone Service) line for this purpose. We depend on our correspondents for local *news* as well as *features*. News taken over the phone is never lengthy; (a correspondent may write up a lengthier version for the next day's paper) and, the newspaper pays the phone bill for this.

Another tip: The Greyhound Bus stops each evening in every one of our outlying towns. A correspondent can take an envelope of copy to the bus station and it will be delivered to us in Lexington by 7 a.m. This is much faster than the regular mail. Once again, the newspaper pays the Greyhound for this service, and supplies the correspondent with special envelopes.

Police and court news make up the biggest bulk of the correspondent's work; news of murders, thefts, fires, court decisions, auto accidents, grand jury indictments. Next in frequency of occurrence, although of greater news value, are the local issues: Are school teachers protesting for higher salaries? Is there a shake-down happening among county officials? Is there controversy over the local water system or zoning practices? This kind of reporting, well-told and accurate, is what the state editor wants and what you, as a writer, can give him.

Club news is least important, although a club project which affects a whole community or a major speech by a county or state official at a club meeting deserves to be reported and might merit feature treatment. If the school superintendent tells the Rotary Club that schools are "going to the dogs," it merits reporting and might lead the alert correspondent to a feature story.

Often routine news stories will lead to features because of a human interest angle or personality involved. For example, routine report of land sales in your area might lead to a historical feature on one of the tracts sold: who first settled it, how often it has changed hands, famous persons who once lived on it, etc.

Major news stories and features should be illustrated with photographs. The newspaper has its own photography lab; all a correspondent has to do, in our case, is send in undeveloped film and captions.

Occasionally you'll get a special assignment. You might be asked to cover a murder trial in your area, report local flood damage or a speech. In fact, any event not significant enough for the wire services to cover in detail or for the editor to dispatch one of his own hard-to-spare reporters may net you an extra assignment.

## A Correspondent's Pay

Most newspapers pay their beginning correspondents from $.10 to $.50 a column inch; the average is about $.15 a column inch. Photographs bring either a flat rate, usually $3-$5, or $1 per column width. Many newspapers start a correspondent on the inch-rate basis but will soon guarantee him a flat monthly salary. The monthly salaries, which range from $50 to $200 depending on the amount of work, usually total quite a bit more than the inch-rate. (That measurement of inches, by the way, is how the term "stringer" got started, since the printer used a length of string to tie the lines of type together and then they were measured.)

Most newspapers buy only first rights to photographs and return them to the correspondent. Many correspondents then sell them to regional or travel magazines or as a keepsake to the persons photographed.

Remember, if you write well, an editor can afford to be generous with you because he needs good writers. They save him from needless rewriting. A typical state editor may be paying as much as $.20 an inch and $100 a month to club (not cub) reporters, funeral directors, high school students, public relations men, police secretaries and others who have no real interest in writing. You will be able to earn top correspondent's pay very easily.

## Some Psychological Satisfactions

Once you have established yourself as a correspondent on a newspaper you are in a very special position. The state editor depends on you, he needs your news to fill his pages. Therefore, you won't get many rejections from the state desk. Your copy may be trimmed, the editor may suggest improvements, but you'll see your copy in the newspaper nearly as often as you see it in your typewriter. To the freelancer somewhat discouraged with rejection slips, this in itself can be satisfying.

## Experience: A Fringe Benefit

A correspondent gets valuable experience getting to know his community, county, region and state. Buried deep in some local news item you might find material for a feature story that has more than local interest, one which you could work into a magazine article or book.

## How To Get Started

(1) Pick out a newspaper. A medium-size daily with a circulation under 100,000 which has regular subscribers in your town is your best choice.

(2) Arrange to see the state editor. Bring him a list of contacts in your town: the local police chief, sheriff, fire chief, undertaker, circuit judge, church leaders, Kiwanis, Chamber of Commerce and Rotary Club leaders, mayor, school superinten-

dent and other important persons. At first you may have to phone these people daily before your editor contacts you; later, when the publicity rolls in, your contacts will phone you.

(3) Get a newspaper style book and any other correspondent's information from the editor; or buy a copy of the *Associated Press Style Book*, ($1.00 from the Associated Press, 50 Rockefeller Plaza, New York, N. Y. 10020).

(4) Don't hesitate if your community already has a correspondent. Many state editors would rather have two in competition with each other to get the news fastest.

For a novelist waiting while his "big one" makes the rounds, a writer doing extensive research for a magazine article, or a housewife who likes to dabble in freelancing, newspaper corresponding can provide a nice supplemental income and a way to keep your time your own.

# Business Anniversaries Mean Freelance Checks for Writers

## Is some company in your community a market?

*by Etna M. Kelley*

EACH YEAR MILLIONS of dollars are spent by organizations celebrating their anniversaries. A typical celebration may include special advertising, various functions (parties, banquets, receptions), a commemorative film, exhibits, distribution of gifts, novelties and souvenirs. But no matter what else is done, *the printed word is usually the major tool used in commemorating the milestone.* Very often there is a company history, in hard or soft covers, or in the form of brochures, folders, booklets. The firm's management sends out releases to the press and to radio and television systems. The company magazine may come out as a special issue, or it may carry a series of articles tied to the birthday. There may be a special anniversary edition of the annual report to shareholders; or a special anniversary booklet may be distributed separately to them.

But even though the volume of anniversary printing is large, it is not nearly so large as it might be if writers would take the initiative of volunteering their services for the occasion, to the celebrating organizations. Much of what appears is handled by the companies' own staffs, or the staffs of their advertising agencies or public relations counsel, who are hard pressed to perform the extra duties related to the milestone, without the additional burden of turning out the writing required for the occasion.

A company celebrating its centennial or other birthday, even the 25th, is newsworthy; and publications in its field or related fields usually welcome—and are willing to pay for—timely articles about it.

No self-respecting editor will publish an article about the 50-year-old XYZ Company, nut and bolt maker, if it is a dull recital of the firm's prosaic history. But if it is a pioneer in its field, the oldest of its kind in the state or region, if it has interesting "firsts" to its credit, if it has made significant contributions to the community—there's a good chance that articles about it may be sold. Usually, the milestone alone is not sufficient as a peg on which to hang the story. But the milestone plus an interesting new development—new product, gift to the community, establishment of a day nursery for employees' children, etc.—that is the formula for an article editors will want.

To get ideas, start by checking the ages of local firms. Don't write off the fairly young ones. I compile annual lists of companies eligible to celebrate major (multiple-of-twenty-five year) anniversaries. These lists indicate that some years are much more favorable than others for the founding and survival of businesses. For instance, there were relatively few 25-year-old firms on the 1966, 1967, 1968 and 1969 Company Birthday Lists, because so few started (and survived) during World War II. On my 1967 list there were only 88 which began in 1942, compared to 211 75-year-olds.

After the end of World War II, many new businesses were founded, and even though the rate of mortality was high, a large number prospered and still exist. My 1971 Company Birthday List of more than 1000 names has on it 64 125-year-olds; 160 100-year-olds; 206 75-year-olds; 207 50-year-olds; and 235 25-year-olds.

It may seem odd that there are almost as many 75-year-old and 50-year-old firms as 25-year-olds. But if you think about the ages of the banks, department stores, insurance companies, food firms, seed houses, funeral establishments in your town, the chances are that you will find most of them are well past the quarter-century mark. Fortunately for those of us who like to sell goods or services, including writing skills, to celebrants, the young firms are likely to observe their birthdays with as much enthusiasm as the older ones.

My *Business Founding Date Directory*, which was published in 1954, listed almost 10,000 firms founded between 1687 and 1915—118 in the 1700s. Some of these 200-year-old, or almost 200-

year-old, firms have disappeared in recent years, but a surprisingly large proportion are still in operation. Twelve founded-in-the-1700s firms are on the 1967 Company Birthday list. A freelance writer searching for article assignments would do well to look into the possibilities among the older organizations in his community, giving priority to those founded in the 1700s—if they exist, but not overlooking those 150, 125 and 100 years old.

The local Chamber of Commerce's Research Department will probably have dates of establishment for member-companies in their cities. If very old, the company is of interest whether or not it is celebrating an anniversary. Another factor is age in relation to the age of the community. In relatively young communities, or even in old ones which were late in becoming industrialized, a 50-year-old firm might be of more interest than one a century old in Boston, Philadelphia, Baltimore or New York.

In asking an editor for an assignment for an article about an old company, a writer should be able to say that he has access to material about its history. If old records, ledgers, catalogs, advertisements, clippings, photographs of founders, early employees, original products, original buildings, have been preserved by the management, the task of the researcher is easier. If the company is still in the hands of the founding family, so much the better. Interviews with long-term employees or those who have retired are often rewarding. But even without these assets, it is often possible to unearth material about the early days of an organization, from which an interesting article may be prepared.

I was once asked to help in the research for a history of a company soon to celebrate its centennial. The owners were not even certain of the year of establishment, though they approximated it. From old city directories, I traced it through several changing locations, as the original owner took on various partners. After several years of existence, it had grown to such proportions that its operations were chronicled at length in the trade paper covering its industry. I got some material from the journal of a historical society in a county where one of its old plants existed. Information about the recent history of the organization was available from the management. The end result was a hard cover book of approximately 300 pages.

In deciding whether to try one's hand at writing about an old company, ask yourself whether you believe you can get enough material to make a really interesting article; or, more to the point, whether you can convince an editor that you can get it. Some companies are of inherent interest: the Borden Company, for example, because of the personality and achievements of its founder, Gail Borden; F.A.O. Schwarz, the New York toy firm; Ferry-Morse, the seed firm. These and many others have been the subjects of articles appearing in national magazines. When Borden celebrated its centennial, much was written about it, and one piece, written before the centennial, was reprinted in the *Reader's Digest*. Schwarz and other interesting toy firms, such as Ideal Toy Corporation (originated the Teddy Bear), have been written about in national magazines, including the *Saturday Evening Post*.

The Sunday magazine supplements of newspapers are particularly good markets for articles about interesting old companies. Passing by the building which houses Samuel French, Inc., the play publisher, and remembering that it was well past 125 years old, I decided that it would make an interesting article, one which would not only tell about the company itself but about the entire amateur theatre movement—since it supplies the plays used by the majority of high schools, churches and other non-Broadway theatrical groups. The firm's president promised his cooperation and I got an assignment from the magazine supplement of the former *New York Herald Tribune*. The article was featured on the front cover, with the title, "2,848 Ways to Serve Ham."

When I compiled my *Business Founding Date Directory*, I added parenthetical comments about companies with distinctive features I considered worth recording. Here are some: "Oldest department store in America" (this refers to Gladding's, in Providence, R.I., founded in 1766, 200 years old this year); "Oldest magic store on North American continent; owned by Houdini at one time"; "Oldest real estate firm in America; operated by 4th and 5th generation descendant of founder"; "Oldest flag makers in America; descendants of founder still associated with firm"; "America's oldest paint manufacturer"; "Oldest rum distillery in America, in continuous operation in Newburyport, always under Caldwell name"; "Oldest ship chandlery in America; operated by 4th and 5th generation of family"; "Oldest corncob pipe manufacturer in the world"; "America's oldest tobacco merchants;" "Oldest window shade manufacturer in America; still manufacturing original brand"; "Oldest printers in New York and oldest firm in city still operating under original name"; "Oldest newspaper of continuous publication in America"; "Oldest auger works in world, it is believed that the holes bored in the wood of the support of the Liberty Bell were made with company's bits."

On a lesser scale, a similar list could be prepared for almost any community: the oldest retailer, oldest manufacturer, oldest financial institution; firms in the same hands since their inception, now operated by third, fourth, etc., generation. Then there are the industrial firsts: first maker of packaged pancake flour; first to make ice cream commercially; first to develop the screw micrometer. In the fields of radio, television, even aviation, the pioneers may be relatively young—but quite proud of their "firsts."

Because of my long experience as a business writer, I tend to think chiefly of the opportunities in selling articles on how companies celebrate their anniversaries to business magazines. It's true that a higher fee would be received for an article about an anniversary-celebrating firm, from a general magazine. But not as many general magazines exist as markets for this type of piece as formerly, so in the long run, the rewards should be better from writing a number of articles about a company's anniversary program and selling them to different business magazines.

As a hypothetical example, let us suppose that I were a writer needing assignments, in a small or medium-size city with several large industrial firms. I'd start a card file on these companies, putting down their founding years, what they produced, and anything else of interest I could learn about them. If they held Open Houses at any time, I'd attend them. I'd try to get literature about them—their "Welcome Booklets" for new employees, their annual reports, their company magazines—if any. When one of them approached an anniversary year, I'd be particularly alert to its activities. (There would be greater likelihood of observance of the multiple-of-twenty-five year birthdays, but I would not write off the possibility of observance of the 40th, 60th, 80th, 85th, 90th, etc.) Well in advance of the anniversary year, I'd try to interview the firm's president, public relations director, or other executive who might have some knowledge of the forthcoming anniversary program. From this executive, I'd try to learn plans. Human nature being what it is, I might be told, "We haven't made any plans as yet." That would not discourage me from inquiring again along the same line a few weeks, or a few months later.

In my own case, the purpose of the interviews would be to show my free-lance writing credits and to ask for cooperation in keeping informed of the anniversary program. But on many occasions, there might be better response to some such proposal as: "Do you need help with the research on the early days of your company? Will you commission me to write an article, or series of articles, about your history, for your company magazine(s)? May I help with other special writing: releases to the press, and to radio and television stations? How about special articles for the publications in your field, or related fields?" With this approach, I'd be asking the company to subsidize my writing. I'd be very sure, though, to make it clear that I wanted to work *with* the company's public relations staff, or outside public relations counsel, if it had these—and that I had no desire to supplant them.

In some instances, the answer would be, "Our own people can handle all the writing we'll need." Then, the writer might ask, "Will you work with me if I get assignments from editors to write about your anniversary program?" Almost invariably, the answer would be "yes." But even if it were not, I'd watch for developments, and if the anniversary celebration had interesting facets, I'd try to get assignments from magazines for stories about them. It's unlikely that management cooperation would be withheld once an editor has shown willingness to publish an article.

When a company is celebrating its anniversary, its public relations department usually sends releases to the press, stating that it has reached the milestone year, that it will stage a party (for employees, customers, suppliers, members of the community, etc.); or that it will dedicate a new building, unveil a time capsule, establish a scholarship fund, etc., to mark the event. And, almost invariably, the release outlines the history of the company, often in a boring fashion. For one reason or another, these hand-outs are generally used, in whole or in part. But what is printed rarely has much meaning to anyone.

But what trade magazine editors would like to have, and are willing to pay for, are the how-to-do-it articles which tell of preparations for the various events occurring during the anniversary year, how they were conducted, and their effect—in other words, case histories. These are clipped and treasured by other companies facing their own anniversary celebrations, by libraries, by public relations organizations.

Another kind of trade magazine article for which there is a demand is the "What-Anniversaries-Mean-to-Your-Industry" type. Photographers, printers, display specialists, souvenir and gift sellers—all want to know how they can sell their products or services to anniversary celebrants, and this information is best given to them through business magazines.

My own evolution as an anniversary specialist came about through writing about anniversaries and related subjects, not because I thought of it myself, but because editors asked me for such articles. The editor of a music magazine asked me to turn in a batch of material for its 50th anniversary edition, based on what was happening in the music field when it started. A photographic magazine's editor wanted to honor a company on its anniversary and asked me to supply some historic material. A man who planned to sell the contents of a famous old wine cellar asked me for material on liquor history. But most of all, the editor of a graphic arts publication used to ask me regularly for articles on company histories and other anniversary literature. I would ask the picture services and printers who specialized in such material to tell me of recently published material in this category, and I was invariably greeted with this question, "Why don't *you* tell *me* who is going to celebrate an anniversary?" So I compiled the list of 10,000 old companies which made up the *Business Founding Date Directory,* and in recent years I have been compiling yearly lists of the following year's birthday companies. But that was not enough. The companies planning to celebrate—and their advertising agencies and public relations counsel—began asking me, "Can you send us copies of your articles on anniversaries?" or "What has been written about anniversary celebrations?" So I found myself preparing small bibliographies and sending tear-sheets of my own articles to a time-consuming and burdensome degree. In self-defense, last year I prepared a bibliography of more than 80 articles, to which I have recently added a supplementary list of another thirteen. I've sold hundreds of copies at $5 apiece.

Skimming through the listings in the bibliography, we find that some articles are of the case history type, outlining a complete program, such as "How to Celebrate a Centennial," commemorating the centennial of the National Banking Act spearheaded by the American Bankers Association in *Advertising and Sales Promotion;* and "It's Borden's Hundredth Year, and 'Sellebration' Is the Word," in *Sales Management.* Others treat specific aspects, such as: "Producing an Anniversary History," "How to Use (Company) Birthday Cakes for Promotion," "How to Design an Anniversary Emblem," "Making Your Anniversary Pay for Itself"—all from *Advertising and Sales Promotion;* "Saying It With Old Sweet Songs," from *Business Week;* "Corporations Invite Shareholders to join in Birthday Celebrations" (about annual reports), from *Direct Advertising;* "Collector's Item—Firms' Anniversary Editions Valuable" (about anniversary supplements and special anniversary editions of newspapers), from *Editor and Publisher;* "Anniversaries—Untapped Sales Potential," from *Printing Magazine;* "Anniversary Gifts: To Whom? What? How?" and "GM Loves Its Birthdays," both from *Sales Management;* "Old Crow's 125th Anniversary Convention," from *Sales Meetings.* Then there are the checklists: "100 Ways Your Bank Can Celebrate," from *Banking;* "1001 Ways to Celebrate an Anniversary," from *Direct Advertising;* "Basic Guide to Anniversary Celebrations," from *Industrial Marketing;* "Having a Birthday—Build a Promotion Around It," from *Sales Management.*

Probably the most valuable type of anniversary article is the case history. Comparatively few are published (except in *Public Relations News*), because their preparation requires in-depth interviewing, time-consuming both for the writer and the company's management. In the preparation of such articles, I have sometimes talked to as many as five company representatives, with top management invariably represented. Sometimes I have attended several events of the anniversary program. There's quite a bit of work entailed, not only for the writer, but for the company's staff, which must furnish pictures (and captions), literature, answers to questions, information about planning—and an appraisal: "Was it worth while? If you had it to do again, would you do it in exactly the same way?" Sometimes it is hard to get a truthful answer, but there is usually some such admission as, "Well, we would not again schedule two important events so close together," "We would have spent more money on souvenirs and less on refreshments"—(or vice versa), or something of the sort.

Getting a specific answer to "Was it all worth while?" is important, because those planning anniversaries want to know this, not just generalities ("It was wonderful") but such information as "We got hundreds of unsolicited thank-you letters," "It built morale; our employees felt that they were the hosts at the Open House and took great pains to make the affair a success." Best of all, "Our sales increased sharply, because of the promotions tied to the birthday."

Even though the research for a comprehensive article on a business anniversary may take quite a bit of time, the silver lining to the cloud is that one may often sell several articles about it. I'm still using material gathered ten years ago. I ask editors to return photographs and printed literature, and use these again and again.

Summing up, to answer the question, "Should I try my hand at writing about business anniversaries?", consider whether you are willing to do the thorough research required. Do you like business history: to look at old advertising, catalogs, ledgers, and even old products and packages? Can you relate these to the present and to the future? If you can, you have in your favor the fact that the field is not overcrowded, and it is usually easy to get a hearing from those responsible for a company's anniversary program. If you write an interesting, comprehensive article, it should have a long life. It should be useful far into the future. I have known people to travel long distances, even across the continent, to talk to those who have conducted successful anniversary programs. A well-written article can serve the same purpose as this kind of a journey.

This article deals chiefly with business anniversaries. But the milestones of colleges, hospitals, charitable institutions, clubs, communities—all can be newsworthy, and could be made the subjects of articles. The anniversaries of inventions (such as the electric light, the radio, the airplane, the telephone; are likely to be celebrated, sometimes by entire industries. At first glance, you might conclude, "If the whole nation celebrates the invention of the electric light, the public relations people will send out reams of material; who would want anything from me?" *If your particular community does something just a bit out of the ordinary, someone will pay you for telling about it.*

I have a slogan, "Any year can be an anniversary year." By this I mean that a company need not wait for the 25th, 50th, 75th, 100th, etc., birthday, but can celebrate the in-between ones. *Seventeen* Magazine made quite a thing out of its own 17th birthday. The Heinz people called attention to their reputation as the "57 Varieties" manufacturer by staging a promotion in 1957. In any given year, there are pioneers, inventors, heroes, to whom anniversary programs may be tied. Some companies celebrate not only their own birthdays, but those of their brands ("We're 86, but our best-selling brand is 50"). Some celebrate the production of the umpteenth car—or can of dog food, or toaster.

Since I write more articles on anniversaries than any other one person, it might seem odd that I should say, "Come on in; the water's fine." But the field is so big that there's room for all. And for those of us who have something to sell to what I call the anniversary market—whether it be printing, souvenirs, jewelry, flowers, cakes, hotel and restaurant facilities, the more the merrier.

# How to Turn Trash into Cash

## Writing & Selling Craft Material for Children

### by M. Mable Lunz

THERE'S REALLY NO genius necessary when it comes to writing handcraft or as they are now called "do it yourself" articles for the children's magazines. A little of the right kind of imagination helps; also helpful but not essential are a couple, or three, children of various ages around to assist you. And if you have a passion for saving useless junk you've got it made . . . you're a writer.

First, the right kind of imagination. That is the kind that can look at a rabbit and see a peanut with pink pipe-cleaner ears and a dab of cotton tail. If you crack a breakfast egg and find you have two tiny igloos, and the empty salt box cut in half lengthwise lined with foil becomes a doll's bath tub with real water no less . . . you've got the right type of imagination. If you haven't got it—develop some.

It's easy. Whenever you go to throw away an empty can, a fancy plastic bottle, a paper cup, anything at all . . . STOP!!! You'll have lots less garbage. That empty tuna can covered with paper or with glued-on shells or flowers might become a plant holder for a Mother's Day gift; turn it upside down and put a piece of cardboard on for a back and you could have a doll's chair; two together, a love seat. The plastic bottle with a plastic foam ball on top for a head could be a doll, (some have the shape for it), add pipe-cleaner arms and easy-to-cut-and-make clothes . . . buttons or thumb tacks make good eyes . . . you take it from there. A paper cup, well let's see . . . if it's a large one you could cut out the top part of one side and make a round hole in the top of the other side to hang over a doorknob for a May basket that can be filled with water and real flowers. If the cup is small you can put on a yarn or ribbon handle.

There's nothing as dead as yesterday's news, but there's

nothing as available as yesterday's newspaper. It could easily become a bulletin board; no, that's not a very good idea; articles that are too large are hard to mail and you must send complete samples of your "how to make its". How about using the newspaper over cardboard for the background of a picture? Frame it with black construction paper and put an outline picture of a clown in the center drawn with heavy black or red crayon or ink. Newspaper mixed with, or strips dipped in starch make good paper-mache. You can mold many clever articles or cover many things with this material.

Children underfoot are a continual source of inspiration and information, be they panpounders, spool stringers, wall decorators, hole diggers or whatever. Make them some kind of drum they can pound, cut them something they can dig with, maybe a part of a plastic bottle that will serve as a scoop, or find them something that's been lying around that they can fill with sand or mold sand in. While they are thus occupied make another, paint or decorate it in some way, write up the directions and sell it. The paper doll set like to make such things as folders or houses to keep their paper dolls in, stands to hold them up, or clothes (my first sale was to JACK AND JILL for paper doll dresses made from muffin cups). For the teen-age doll enthusiast doll furniture is always welcome. My doll furniture sales have been for furniture made from popsicle sticks, molded egg boxes, cottage cheese cartons, wood and hair pins with sponge seats, thread spools and muffin cups. Dolls also need hangers, hats, hat boxes and handbags.

### Boys: A Special Breed

I learned from one editor that boys aren't about to spend their time making tie pins or clasps, but I have found they'll make badges, marble bags, dragons, gas stations and equipment such as pumps, etc., various things they can use as background around their electric trains, animal cages and animals from almost any kind of material, nuts, shells, acorns, pine cones, paper, cardboard. Boys will also make things like name plates for desks, or bicycles or tricycles and house numbers. Incidentally, boys' articles are much harder for editors to obtain than those for girls, so help yourself to this market!

Now you have several drawers and a closet full of useless junk like tin cans in fifteen sizes, egg cartons in three shapes, empty thread spools, popsicle sticks, berry baskets, newspapers, buttons, nuts and nut shells, fancy wrapping paper, cards, empty wax paper tubes, boxes of all shapes and sizes, all kinds of empty bottles and bottle tops, pieces of material, bits of lace, ribbon, yarn, foil, sea shells, that piece of ski rope you cut off when it broke . . . *so you moved your clothes into his closet.* You do want to be a writer?

Still need some ideas about where to get ideas? Take each month and think of the holidays, and the gifts and cards and party favors that you can make for this special month. Gifts for Mother's Day, Father's Day, Christmas, Easter, cards for each occasion, place cards for Thanksgiving, maybe an easy-to-make cornucopia for a table decoration, all kinds of Christmas decorations for the house, or the tree. Remember, for special months, material must be sent four to six months before the day for which it is intended.

Don't overlook school pennants or pins, book covers, or anything that can be made in school colors and worn or carried to school. Another thing, have you ever noticed how much like a tiny football a pecan looks?

Games are another source of ideas. WEE WISDOM used a table-top shuffleboard, made from a long piece of shelf paper, with pencils for pushers and buttons for disks, a game that could be rolled up and put away for future use. A croquet set made from miniature marshmallows and pipe cleaners also went to WEE WISDOM, and we used ours for a couple years before it got tossed out.

Take a hammer and pound a pop bottle top flat. What does it remind you of? A picture frame, a pin; take out the cork, what could you make from a cork circle or two or three? Now that's an idea . . .why don't you try it? You could put it together with popsicle sticks or pipe cleaners, or the bottom of one of those plastic berry baskets might work.

Did your sample turn out okay? Good . . . now you're ready to write.

## How To Submit Your Article

Suppose you had made a clown on newspaper with a black construction paper frame. Opposite is how you might write the ms.

CLOWN PICTURE

by

Your Name

Take a piece of black construction paper. Draw a line all around the outside of it one inch in from the edge. Cut a piece of cardboard about one-half inch smaller all around than the construction paper. Now take a piece of newspaper the same size, put a little paste or glue along the edge of the cardboard and paste on the newspaper. Punch a hole with a paper punch on each side of the covered cardboard about one-quarter inch in from the sides and about two inches from the edge. Punch another hole on each side about one-half inch below the first hole. Put a piece of string through the two holes on one side and make a knot in back, make the string long enough to hang up the picture when it is finished and put it through the holes on the other side and tie it in a knot in back.

Use black or red crayon or ink, to outline the clown head on the newspaper. Use the head of the clown shown in the picture, or make clown of your own. You may want to make several different clowns and then choose the one you like best to put in your frame. Be sure to make the outlines very dark so you can see the clown's face if you are across the room.

Now cut the center out of the piece of black construction paper along the lines you made, and glue the frame over the picture so that all the edges are completely covered. When the glue is dry your clown picture is ready to hang.

Always write the directions for making your article clear and as short and to the point as possible. No flowery language, no adjectives describing your brain child, just straight step-by-step directions, telling exactly what you have made and how you made it.

The article on page 60 is less than 300 words. Editors appreciate brevity. On regular typing paper put your name and address complete with zip code number in the upper left-hand corner. Center your title, by, and name on single lines double spaced starting about one third of the way down from the top of the paper. Skip four to six spaces and type your article double spaced. Leave at least an inch margin and an inch at the bottom of each page. If you need a second page put the article title at the top and page 2. Make simple drawings of the project. A clown outline on a small scale to show one-inch blocks of the finished picture is good, also show a piece of construction paper with one-inch line drawn around, marking the center to be cut out, and one of the completed project. These drawings may be crude but make them clear with dark ink and use a ruler to make straight lines. Mark any measurements necessary on the diagrams. Most magazines have artists who will make the diagrams that appear with your article in the magazine.

You may send several articles to the same editor at one time, three or four, up to about six. Pack your samples carefully to prevent breakage in mailing. Enclose enough postage for the return of your material. Articles and a cover letter may be enclosed in the package if you mark "letter enclosed" on the outside.

Keep a carbon copy of every article you write and when you have one package in the mail start working on another. Keep a record of where your articles are. Send them to only one editor at a time. If you have several article packages out in the mail at the same time you have that many more chances of receiving a check.

Make your articles original; not something you saw somewhere and changed slightly. Editors read and see the same things you do, so don't waste your time and postage.

In making articles from cardboard, paper, macaroni, even wood, poster paint or water color in bright colors gives a pretty effect, covers well and is readily available. I use poster paint on many things, especially the pressed egg cartons which is one of my favorite construction materials because of the interesting shapes that can be cut from it. It glues readily, paint covers it easily, and it dries quickly; holes can be poked in the parts with little effort and pipe cleaners inserted. I call this my cut, poke and paint material. Another material I use often is the tubes wax paper or toilet tissue come rolled upon. This can be cut into rings or sections to make anything from dragons to Christmas candles or angels.

## A Special Caution!

One word to the wise: don't make anything that is sharp, or needs tools that would be dangerous for children to use. If wood must be sawed, it is good to put in your directions such instructions as, "Ask Dad to help you cut two pieces of wood the size of the pattern." Other good directions are, "Ask mother to give you an old pair of scissors that you can use to cut the wire;" or, "lay a piece of newspaper on the table and set your paint cans and pieces on it, then when you are finished you can roll up the paper and throw it away."

You can make a scrapbook of ideas by clipping pictures of furniture, dresses, animals, toys, anything that trips your imagination, write a note along side the clipping or you will forget why you clipped it. Picture of a squirrel, (notes could read), try with paper tube, knot pieces of yarn on pipe cleaner to make bushy, bendy tail.

Don't fail to take advantage of new products or new packages that make good handcraft materials. Paper companys especially, often make new products, change colors, or add designs to napkins, towels, tissues, or toilet paper. One toilet tissue is even made with white on one side and a color on the other and it smells good too. Could it be twisted, pleated, tied in knots, for flowers, doll dresses, paper doll dresses? Now there's an idea ... you see ... there's really no genius necessary!

# Freelance Job Opportunity: Advertising Writing

## *Is there a local retail business looking for your writing skills?*

*by Mary Louise Foley*

THAR'S GOLD IN them thar garbage cans!

It's no secret in the advertising world that today's newspaper becomes tomorrow's refuse wrapper, but before it disguises the orange peels and coffee grounds, the advertising in that newspaper has played an important part in the lives of thousands; motivating, stimulating, nagging, encouraging and too often ordering them to buy, rent, trade, repair, visit, enjoy . . . you name it! . . . you'll find an ad to spur you on. The fact that a writer's creation should suffer such an early and humiliating demise is discouraging to some, and those of you who are not hungry may turn the page while the rest of us greedy souls plod through a short course in the field of freelance advertising writing.

In the past 13 years, the dizzy world of Sale! Spectacular! Vote! and Hurry! has helped this writer fend off medical bills, buy spur-of-the-moment dresses, cover-up mathematical overdrafts on our joint checking account (I can neither add nor subtract, but I love to write . . . checks) and has brought me into contact with a great many talented people. It has broadened my appreciation of sales techniques and given me a nodding acquaintance with art and layout design. But without doubt, the most valuable intangible asset I have acquired is discipline.

The discipline of writing for a deadline is a quality that every professional writer, esthetic or commercial, must have to succeed. Freelance advertising requires creativity and discipline in equal measures.

Where does a writer go to ferret out freelance jobs in advertising?

1) *Department Stores:* Notorious for understaffed advertising departments, these should be number one on your list. The pay is somewhat lower than you might get from an agency or individual retailer, but once you become a "regular" you are on call for both pre-planned promotions and last minute emergencies.

2) *Advertising Agencies:* On gaining a new account, agencies will often take one of their senior writers off general copy and put him on a special planning staff to map out a "Look" for the new advertiser. This leaves an opening for a freelancer to work on an established account, for which precedent has been set and an image already established. This sounds callous, but the freelancer must be willing to accept the leftovers, while the "plums" go to regular staff. The advertising freelancer runs interference, works under constant pressure and pioneers no new territory . . . until, he proves his ability. However, once you have satisfied your accounts that you can write creatively, take orders and work within a provided framework, possibilities are good that you will be handed an entire promotion to execute. It is always egotistically rewarding to learn that "your" 10-day sale topped all records for the advertiser; and monetarily rewarding in repeat jobs.

3) *Political campaigns:* Brochures, slogans, campaign letters, fund-raising speeches . . . there is a multitude of writing jobs available to the freelancer in state and local campaigns. Contact campaign headquarters.

4) *Individual businesses, Real Estate Firms:* Many businesses are too small to pay the retainer often required by an advertising agency and could use an experienced writer to set up an advertising program. Real estate companies sometimes hire freelancers to do all their classified ads! Hardly inspiring work, but it will buy typewriter ribbons to get you through your next novel.

5) *Shopping Centers:* Most large shopping centers have a public relations staff to plan their promotions, but periodically the writing chores for special sales and activities mushroom appreciably. Having your name in the freelance writer's file could mean one day's work a month, or more.

Well, that's where to go. Here's what to take.

*Sample copy*—slanted toward the merchandise or services in which your prospective employer deals.

1) A department store is not interested in savings and loan advertising. They want to know if you can sell 1,300 spring dresses at $15 each, because their fashion buyer didn't believe the weatherman when he predicted snow in April.

2) Agencies—try them on institutional copy. Banks, restaurants and housing subdivisions are good areas to cover.

3) Political Campaigns—Walk up to a candidate with six catchy slogans (based on information you have culled from local newspaper accounts of his platform; and you're off and running on a successful campaign. Immediacy is of the essence. Note too, that non-incumbents provide better opportunities for freelancers. Men already in office always seem to have agencies handling their campaigns.

4) Individual Businesses, Real Estate Firms—Keep a newspaper file of previous advertising published by these accounts. Find out what their slogans are. Every business has at least one line that is repeated in each ad, a line very dear to someone (thought up, no doubt, by the wife of the owner). Don't fight city hall. Incorporate that idea with yours in your presentation. When you've landed the job and are signing his proofs, you can tactfully approach him with a new slogan.

5) Shopping Centers—Here is one deviation from the foregoing rule of "don't rock the boat." Shopping centers that are large enough to have a Public Relations staff are always looking for new ideas to attract customers. Come in with a "hot" one and you've found a home! Art shows on the mall, Italian street fairs, carnivals, cake decorating contests, beauty pageants . . . there's no end to the sparkle you can put in that P.R. man's eye with a practical, workable promotion. I recall one publicity plan that I helped organize several years ago, in which an airplane exhibit was planned at a suburban shopping center, with private aircraft companies participating. Free coupons were available at all the stores in the center and the winners of the drawing were to receive their choice of two private flying lessons or a two-hour aerial tour of the region. The obstacles were tremendous. One, in particular. How were the planes to get to the concrete parking lot of the shopping center? Fly them in,

of course. But the approach planned was short and we ended up bringing them in at 4 A.M. with local police setting up roadblocks on adjacent streets to facilitate landings. The fire department had crews stationed at the scene. F.A.A. clearance was obtained and flight patterns cleared with the local airport. Deputies were hired to guard the aircraft against possible vandalism when the center closed at night. The show ran three days and was a howling success, with curious customers scrambling to get a firsthand view of light aircraft and staying to leave their money with the merchants, but I cite this example to point up the obstacles that could arise if you put yourself out on a limb without carefully researching all angles.

Here's how to prepare written advertising copy.

In radio and TV copy, you are limited by time. In printed copy, you are limited by space. Each ad you see in the paper has been designed by a layout artist. The layout flatly tells you how much you can write and where you should put it. It tells you where the art will be in relation to the copy, how many lines of copy you may write and how long those lines must be. You are courting trouble if you argue with a layout artist or change the layout.

Layout artists labor under two inflexible rules.

Rule #1) Make the art as large as possible and the copy space miniscule. This rule applies when the buyer gives you 18 factual selling points that must appear in the ad.

Rule #2) Shows one pair of shoes in a full page, with indications for 24 lengthy lines of copy. For this ad, the buyer has provided you with the following copy information . . . "Shoe Sale, all sizes, $9.99 pair."

Layout artists are not nasty people. They're just independent and like it or not, they plan the ads!

Since you do not have the services of a layout artist to prepare your brochure, you may don this cap for yourself. Select a sample ad from your newspaper, and using a large piece of tracing paper or tissue paper, *roughly* outline the artwork and *carefully* rule in the copy blocks. Since the layout will be your "blueprint," be accurate in measuring line lengths and heights of the copy blocks. Using the newspaper ad as reference, count the number of characters (letters and spaces) on an average line, set your typewriter margin accordingly and compose your own copy to fit the space provided. For practice purposes, it is easier to use an ad in which the copy areas are squared off, with lines of equal length.

Almost every firm involved in the use of printed matter has a favored type face; a pre-determined "look" over which the copywriter has no control. When you are assigned a job, your employer will provide you with a type book, published by the newspaper or printing shop that will set and print your copy. This type book shows the type faces or styles that are available in their composing room, and each type face in the book has a matching chart to tell how many characters will fit in lines of varying lengths. An afternoon spent with "Specimens of Type Faces," published by the U.S. Government Printing Office and available in depository libraries, would be profitable to a novice seeking a niche in freelance advertising. This book will give you some idea of the varying sizes and styles of types.

Type is measured in "points." For example, a type face can be available in 6 pt., 8 pt., 10 pt., with some styles going as high as 120 point. The type size you are now reading is 10 point; the style is Caledonia.

Copy line lengths for printed matter are measured in picas. Pica rulers are available at most art shops, but it's not necessary to make that investment for most advertising departments can supply you with one, when you get an assignment. For mechanical practice purposes, you can convert inches to picas by multiplying by six. (One inch equals six picas).

Let's compose an ad for an imaginary coffemaker, using a 10 pt. (type size) Vogue Light (type face) in a five-line copy block, with each line 12 picas in length.

Checking the Vogue Light chart in the type book, we find that a 12-pica line will hold 32 characters in 10 point size.

The copy to be published goes on the left hand side of the page; instructions to the composing room go on the right.

Gleaming, stainless steel coffee-maker by Sandley brews 10 perfect cups every time! Regulator light signals when done. Unit carries 1-year manufacturer's warranty.

(10 vogue light tailor in 12 picas)

The above is an illustration of "tailored" copy; copy that is both flush right and flush left. It fits in a rectangular or squared-off area. It is permissible to fudge a little on line lengths; for instance, a line with a great many "i" and "l" letters will hold more characters than one with a great many "o" and "m" letters. I try to keep within one character of the chart indications.

Sometimes copy lines will curve to fit around artwork. Your layout may then call for lines of differing lengths. Each line must be measured, character count determined (remember, when on assignment you will have a type book to assist you) and copy typed as follows:

Gleaming, stainless steel coffeemaker          (10 vogue light,
by Sandley brews 10 perfect cups very time.   stagger right,
Regulator light signals when done.            flush left, per
Manufacturer's 1-year                         layout)
warranty on each unit.

Incidentally, your typewritten copy is always set up with a flush margin. The layout and your instructions to the composing room will indicate how it is to appear in the published ad. When your copy is written, circle the copy blocks on the layout and number them. Now, in the left-hand margin of your type-written copy, number each item to correspond with its number on the layout. The composing room will get both layout and typed copy and will set up the ad from this information. Always use a black pencil to mark up your copy and layout, to avoid confusion with the composing room's colored markings.

(These mechanics are not necessary on a *sample* brochure. Your interviewer will be more interested in copy content than in your instructions to the composing room. But, the mechanics are very important when you are given an assignment, for without them the layout is nothing but a maze of lines and sketches.)

On receiving a job, ask the layout artist to indicate type sizes and styles on the layout; for the type you set will paint a picture just as much as the artists's drawings and the two must complement each other.

Study the ads in your local paper. Notice the headlines. Are they black, heavy-set type? Are they all caps or all lower case? Italic, perhaps. And what about prices? Prestige institutions often "sink" their prices right into the copy block. You have to search to find the price, and for good reason. The price is *not* a selling point! Sale ads, on the other hand, have the prices blatantly screaming at you from the top of the page. Copy content depends on both the institution and the merchandise. Each writer has his own style, which must be applied within the framework of the advertiser's image.

Some examples of frameworks are:

*Action*—for sportswear, sporting equipment, mechanical toys. These are handled with a light flair, active words, brief sentences, catchy headlines.

*Institutional*—for services, banks, hotels. Give these a prestigious approach with interesting, factual copy.

*Fashion*—furs, custom and quality apparel. Snob appeal enters the picture here. Prices won't sell these goods. Give them stately, luxurious treatment.

*Hard lines*—linens, hardware, china. These are utilitarian items. Make people *need* them, with a straightforward, serviceable approach.

Play the scene to suit the audience and you'll be successful in advertising!

What about money? This is hard to predict on a national scale, but depending on the size of the city and the availability of competent writers, a freelancer could earn from $2.50 to $10 per hour. Some one-time-only jobs, such as political pamphlets, are arranged on a flat fee. Certainly after you have proved your worth to a firm, you could renegotiate salary.

One of the greatest joys of advertising writing, especially to young mothers who are trying to combine career with raising a family, is the asset of being able to work at home. While some firms will ask you to work in their offices; others will strictly forbid it, because of personnel insurance regulations. (Freelancers are not covered under employee insurance.)

Ninety percent of my own freelance work is done at home. I keep an accurate account of the hours spent on a job and send out billing monthly.

"We don't want it good . . . we want it tomorrow" is one of the unfunny funnies you hear in an advertising office, but the discipline of a deadline *is* a spur to creativity . . . and a sideline in freelance advertising may help push you toward that typewriter every night.

Today's advertising . . . tomorrow's garbage wrapper . . . and next week's check. Yup! Thar's gold in them thar garbage cans!

# Getting Started in Comedy Writing

**A few years ago, a 23-year old freelance gag writer approached Jack Paar with some ideas. His name: Dick Cavett. Now look where he is!**

*by Eugene Perret*

THE MOST DIFFICULT step in any new career is the first one. Suppose one has the talent, the desire, and the persistence. How does he go about letting the rest of the world know about it? Perhaps a recount of how I got my start will serve as an example to others who would like to travel the same path.

The first question I had to ask was, "Is the material I write really funny?" My answer: if someone is willing to pay money for it, it's funny! I bought a book on writing short humor for magazines which included a representative market list. I devoured the book in a day, mailed a set of twelve gags to one of the buyers, and received a check for five dollars. Since the book only cost $4.95, I began a new career and made five cents to boot.

Selling material to the magazines is a good way to test your material. It forces you to write gags fairly regularly, it gives polish to your material before you offer it to a comedian, and those incoming checks will be valuable encouragement. Also, the rejection slips you receive will make you feel like a professional.

Three tips may cut down the percentage of rejections you receive:

1. Send a respectable amount of material to each buyer. You'll find that the editor often likes the gags that you were so-so over, and the gags that you're crazy about won't sell. I send anywhere from six to twelve gags out in one mailing.

2. Send each gag on a separate sheet of paper, preferably a

3 x 5 sheet. Have your name and address in full in the upper lefthand corner on each sheet. (You can have a rubber stamp made for two or three dollars. It will save you plenty of time.) Remember, the editor is working for a living, too. If he receives ten or twelve gags of equal value, he'll chose the one that creates the least work for him. If yours is on a separate sheet, he can pluck it out and return the unused ones. Easier for him; a sale for you.

3. Always enclose a stamped, self-addressed (use that rubber stamp again) envelope. Again, editors are human. If you keep making life easier for them, they have to like you.

But let's get back to my own personal experience, trying to get into show business: The checks were encouraging, but they weren't leading directly to writing comedy material for performers. So I watched every comedian on television that I possibly could. I concentrated on Bob Hope. I did this because Hope's material is about the purest form of comedy available. It is not affected by gimmicks as that of many other comedians. Studying Jerry Lewis' material as such would be almost useless for a gag writer because so much of the comedy comes from Jerry himself and not from the material.

Hope's routine would be funny if you read it in a newspaper the following day. Jerry Lewis' material would be lifeless in a newspaper. It would lack that inimitable Lewis mimicry. Since I was dealing with comedy that could be put on paper, I analyzed Hope's material. I taped several of his television shows, typed his scripts and studied them until I began to have a feel for his style and pattern. Then I wrote several scripts and at last had something on paper to take to a comedian.

## Start Close to Home

Probably every town has its Mr. Show Business. That entertainer who stands head and shoulders above the rest in the same area. In my hometown of Philadelphia, that happened to be Mickey Shaughnessy. Mickey knew everyone who had anything to do with show business in Philly. I reasoned that if anyone knew whom I should contact, it was Shaughnessy. I called Mickey and gave him my story straight. I've written material; I think it's good; I'd like someone in the business to look it over, give me an opinion and tell me where to go from here. Mickey invited me to send the material to his home address. He read it, thought it showed promise, and introduced me and my material to several people. This, of course, is not the end of my story. It's only the first step. But you'll find, as I did, that it's the first step that's important. *Take the first step,* and you'll find your way after that.

There are two important lessons for beginners I've found since writing comedy. First, there is a *tremendous* demand for good comedy material. Television has created a large market for the comedy writer because it uses up an enormous amount of material, and because it exposes the public to very good entertainment. The public has become so conditioned to high-class entertainment, it won't tolerate inferior material. Consequently, all comedians need good comedy material.

Secondly, all comedians are willing to look at comedy routines. If you approach entertainers courteously, and make it as convenient as possible for them to see your writing, you'll find most of them will be agreeable. It's tougher to get to them in New York or Hollywood but it has been done.

Keeping these thoughts in mind then, let's see how you can contact Mr. Show Business in your hometown. Begin simply by talking it up. Let your friends and your associates know that you have a script and you're trying to contact this person. Chances are you'll run across someone who may know his home address or his phone number. (The chances aren't that slim. That's how it happened to me.) At the same time, keep an eye on the theatrical section of the local paper. Sooner or later, you'll find he's appearing at one of the clubs in town. Call the club and ask for him. The front desk will generally connect you with the back stage phone. If he's not there, find a convenient time to call back.

If for some reason you can't contact the comedian by phone, try sending a special delivery letter addressed to him at the club asking him to contact you.

Perhaps the simplest method is to go to the club, catch his act, and then send a message to him backstage, via your waiter, that you are a comedy writer and would like to talk to him.

Always mention that you have comedy material . . . this is the key that opens the door.

Certainly, people in show business guard their privacy and it's easy to understand why. For this reason it is sometimes difficult to contact them. However, if you try often enough and always with courtesy, you should succeed.

Suppose now your town has no Mr. Show Business, or at least, none that you know of. What then? Keep an eye on the local papers again for news that some comedian will be in your town. Make a note of it and begin a campaign to contact him and meet him while he's in town. Exhaust every angle until you come up with something definite. You might begin by calling the person who wrote the column. In this case, use your ingenuity. This is why that third element—persistence—is so important.

Remember this—don't be awed by the person's reputation. Generally you'll find in show business, the bigger they are, the nicer they are. These performers have all suffered through many lean years as entertainers. Most of them are sympathetic to beginners.

When I was beginning as a writer, I contacted Marty Allen and Steve Rossi, two promising comedians who are now at the top among comedy duos. They were appearing at a New Jersey night spot, and I wanted to show them a record script I had written. They invited me to see the show, they read my material, and offered helpful advice. My routines weren't their style, but they were willing to listen and help.

Finally, become a regular reader of VARIETY. The vaudeville section lists the night clubs of the major cities and who is appearing where. When you run across the name you're looking for, send a special delivery letter right away or place a person-to-person call. Telephone information will gladly supply the phone number and address of the club you're after.

This may sound like a roundabout way of selling comedy, but remember it's only the first step. Things become much simpler after that. I now write regularly for four comedians. With two of them I hold contracts which give me a percentage of their contract price—the price they receive for working a particular night club or television show. The others look at material that I write exclusively for them, and pay me a set price for the gags they accept. These are the regular customers. There are also comics who come to me with an idea which I will work into a finished routine for a set price. I also have speculative work—ideas which I work up and hope to find a buyer for.

There is no standard price or contract for a freelancer. It depends on what you hope to accomplish. In the beginning, you work for next to nothing to gain experience and a reputation as a good comedy writer. However, when you have so many assignments that your time is at a premium, you cannot afford to work unless the price is right.

After you have taken that important first step, maintain the momentum. Let the world know about your good fortune. You are now part of a glamorous field—entertainment. People will now be interested in YOU. You'll discover that comedy writing is a great conversation piece. People want to know whom you've met; what are they *really* like; are they as funny offstage as they are on? Capitalize on this interest. Write to your local newspapers and tell them your story. Write to the theatrical columnists in your town. Contact the radio and television interview shows. You'll be pleasantly surprised at the "celebrity" you've become yourself.

After I had signed my first contract, I toyed with the idea of writing a letter to the editor of the industrial house organ where I worked . . . a paper that was printed for the employees only. I shelved this idea several times. It seemed too much like patting myself on the back and I was sure the editor would spot it as such. Finally, something prompted me to write. That letter has probably done more for my career than any other single event.

The plant paper did a feature story on my work. The local paper picked it up and did a feature story on my writing. The editorial columnist on the same paper devoted a full column to my career. The list just kept growing until I was mentioned several times in the best theatrical column in Philadelphia—a column which some pros have tried for years to crack. It reached a personal climax for me when I saw my name mentioned in one of the chatter columns in VARIETY. This publicity led to several radio interviews and eventually made it easier for me to begin my own career as a comedian.

## The Comedy Performer

I really wanted to become a comedian. Comedy writing served as my apprenticeship. It has been a fascinating, and financially-rewarding apprenticeship. For those of you who do not wish to become performers, it can be a financially-rewarding career.

However, I always intended to use comedy writing as a stepping stone to performing. It has taught me many things.

One of the first lessons was that anyone who had reached success as a comedian, worked hard . . . and continues to work hard. Bob Hope, one of the greatest, spends many hours rehearsing and perfecting his routines. Phyllis Diller, today's best stand-up comedienne, spent nine years polishing her material and delivery. This lesson prompted me to begin to develop a style and delivery of my own.

There is no way of gaining experience before an audience except speaking before an audience. I began a campaign to get some speaking engagements. I volunteered to emcee any function I could find—from Cub Scout banquets to retirement parties. I would begin each show with a short monolog—long enough to test my material and delivery, but not long enough to ruin the evening if it bombed.

I worked most of these events for nothing. I was making money as a writer, and I welcomed the opportunity to polish my delivery.

After several of these shows, the style began to jell; I found myself a bit more at ease; and, to my surprise, I had even built up a small following.

I don't mean to oversimplify. For the three years or so that I consciously worked on my own comedy style, I made several mistakes and I missed opportunities, but I learned many lessons, too. For instance, I had done several shows for one group of people with remarkable success. I always aimed my gags directly at them and included a great deal of "inside stuff." Once, when they asked me to do a half-hour show for them, I contacted a sound man who agreed to tape the show with the possibility that it would be made into a long-playing record. This was all done on speculation. It seemed to be a sure-fire hit. The audience had seen my material and laughed hard at it before. I was sure of tremendous audience reaction. However, because we hoped to sell this tape, I had to write my material to exclude any "inside" gags.

The show, in a word, was disastrous. When these people saw me come on stage and heard me talk about the weather, television, and several other general topics, they looked at me as if they had never seen me before. So a mistake was made; an opportunity was lost (I haven't approached the sound man since); but a valuable lesson was learned.

I knew then that my material had to be aimed directly at the audience. I've exploited that lesson ever since. As a matter of fact, I advertise my talks as "Custom-tailored Comedy." I'm not the kind of comedian that appears before a group of sales engineers and talks about how fat my mother-in-law is. I appear before sales engineers and talk about customer complaints or specification changes. I try to talk about the things the audience wants to hear.

These are the lessons I've learned. My comedy is far from perfected, but I've picked up a delivery and a stage presence that is now marketable, at least on a local level. Soon, I hope, it may reach a national level.

You can begin a comedy career or a speaking career by doing as much speaking as you possibly can. Make "volunteer" your middle name. You're not doing it for nothing; you're getting an education.

Concentrate first on your stage presence. Try to look and sound like a professional while you're on stage. The only way of accomplishing this is hard, missionary-zeal, rehearsal.

Work next on finding your character. By trial and error discover which type of material the audience likes most to hear from you. My forte seems to be talking to the audience about themselves or things they're familiar with. Your character may come across best talking about your mother-in-law. No comedian becomes top-notch until he discovers his character.

When your material and delivery have passed the incubator stage, it's time to line up some paying appearances. (The same is true here as was true with comedy writing . . . if they're willing to pay for it, it's funny.) You'll make things easier by getting as much free advertising about yourself as possible. People are more inclined to pay for a speaker if they've seen his picture in the paper.

Next, pay for some advertising. Have a flyer made up telling about your routine. Pick a few of your more popular gags and list them on your flyer. Mail these out to your prospective clients, who may be program chairmen at associations in your town that hire speakers regularly—exchange clubs, writer's clubs, athletic associations. Also, keep a watch on the local papers again. When you spot a banquet coming up, contact the program chairman.

Remember, though, that your most important advertisement is YOU. Do a good job. On second thought, do an excellent job. A beginner has to stand out. If you do a superb job, it will lead to other engagements.

Neither writing nor performing is an easy road. But with talent, desire, and persistence it is a navigable road. If this article helps you take that *first step*, you'll find it's also a fascinating, enjoyable road.

## Pay for Comedy Writers

It is very hard to be specific about payment for comedy writers. Each writer has to set his own standards. However, let me outline my experiences as a guide to other beginners. My first contract was with an established comedian, signed to a first rate New York Agency. He is not a "big name" of the Danny Thomas-Joey Bishop class, but a perennial favorite who makes a comfortable living from performing. My contract with him states that I will furnish a reasonable amount of material weekly—all original—and that I shall receive 5% of his gross for each engagement. There is a clause which states that if he works for over $2500 a week, my percentage is escalated to 7½ %.

I have a contract with a local comedian. This performer is just beginning his career and plays in small clubs, private parties, banquets, etc. He is strictly a weekend performer at the present time. My duties with him are basically the same, except that my return is a straight 7½ %.

I work also with Phyllis Diller. My work with her is purely speculative. I work up a routine consisting of approximately 30 gags; she chooses any number at all from these and pays at the rate of 5 dollars per gag. I have been averaging 50 dollars a routine.

There are three very different types of writing. Each has its own financial return and its own return as far as experience is involved. Since I wish to be a performer, money is not the only variable. Writing for the New York comic brings the greatest financial return. He gets from $30,000 to $50,000 per year of which I get over 5%. It also brings me into some of the finest clubs to see the top stars in the night club field. Working with the local comic brings very small money, but it affords me the opportunity to see some very bad performers, and to learn by their mistakes. This gentleman happens to be highly talented. If his career should swing upward, mine will also. It's also an opportunity to test some of my material with a performer who needn't be quite so discerning as the one in a higher-priced night club.

Working with Phyllis Diller can be as lucrative as I choose it to be. I can write as much as I want or as little as I want. The burden of meeting a deadline is never present. It has the reward of having your material accepted by the tops in the field. Also, there is always the possibility that the material may impress her to the degree that when a steady writing job is available, I may be considered.

Other assignments may present themselves. There have to be analyzed as to the time and effort they will take and then priced accordingly. I have asked prices of $10 a minute, $2 per joke, or $60 per routine (generally around 30 gags).

As for maximums and minimums, writing for a television show is highly lucrative—the minimum is now around $600 per show, but some writers have been reported to receive as high as $15,000 per show. The average, I would guess, ranges from $1,000 to 1,500. The comedian often buys the *idea*, not necessarily a "good joke." At higher rates, you might have to agree to a certain amount of rewriting.

Comedy performers also receive a wide range of prices. Most of the small local night clubs offer from $65 to $125 per weekend. A weekend, of course, may include as many as six shows. Performers with a Las Vegas showplace may earn $35,000 per week. Top comedy performers have earned $7,500 for speaking at banquets.

I have stayed away from the small local clubs for the time being because I feel that my comedy style is a little too sophisticated for these audiences. I have concentrated on building up a circuit of banquets and doing shows for organizations, for example, the Knights of Columbus, writers' clubs, the Masons, etc. My fee for these assignments is generally slightly higher than one dollar per minute . . . a one-hour show for $70. This is not high. Most of the organizations pay this gladly, and I still consider myself in training.

The New York comedian I work for has played most of the top night clubs across the country. He generally gets second billing to the singing star. His price ranges now from $1,250 to $2,000 per week. Of course, were always trying to get more!

*—Eugene Perret*

# Make Your Vacation Pay for Itself

## With pre-planning, a camera and the information in this chapter

*by Paul H. Fugleberg*

WHAT'S THAT? The cost of living is putting the old squeeze on the family budget to the extent that you're thinking of canceling the family vacation next year?

If your family is like ours, it's easy to see how the thought comes to a frazzle trying to make ends meet, but inflation takes its toll of the budget.

But, if you're fortunate enough to be at least a part-time free-lance writer, you can still afford that vacation trip. All you have to do is to "write and shoot" your way through it.

It's fun, too, and it can make the entire trip more enjoyable and interesting for everyone. All it takes is a little bit of advance research of places you'll be going to and through; a few extra stops to pick up more data and take the right pictures; and an imaginative, keen, observing eye.

The combination can be worked into a vacation that will pay for itself.

How to go about it? Well, after having decided where you'll go, map out a tentative route. Select meal, rest and overnight stops. Then, look a little closer. Are there any apparent scenic attractions en route—just a couple of miles or so off the beaten track—that you think might be interesting places to visit? Make a list of them from which to establish later priorities.

Local chambers of commerce are ideal sources for information on attractions in their areas. They'll gladly furnish pamphlets, accommodations listings, listings of things to do, sites to see, places to go.

Every community has its prides and joys—they can be museums, famous landmarks, unusual buildings, elaborate park systems, newly completed civic projects, community celebrations, etc. All have possible story angles to them.

Write to the daily or weekly newspapers in some of these communities and explain you'll be visiting the area at a certain time with intentions of doing an article on attractions in that area. Ask for sample copies of their most recent Progress Edition or Vacation Guide. Cost, if any, will be minimal as many newspapers provide free samples if it will help advertise the community.

From those samples you'll get leads on an even wider selection of topics—plus an introduction to good background sources if you decide to delve deeper into details on a certain story.

Just reviewing this material as it comes in can provide considerable amounts of family fun and discussion—and usually some lively debate occurs when it comes down to the point of deciding priorities.

The time comes to finally hit the road . . . just a reminder: Don't forget to pack the camera and lots of film. We forgot once, and had to backtrack 50 miles to get our "meal ticket."

The camera, incidentally, doesn't have to be an expensive one. We use an old Minolta Autocord with shutter speeds up to 1/500th, and lens openings from 3.5 to 22. We find Tri-X the best film to use because of its versatility—inside or out, with or without flash. A second camera, a 25-year-old Zeiss, is usually loaded with color film.

Once on the road, innumerable additional photo and story possibilities become evident. The only limit is your imagination . . . and the driver's tolerance of requests for sudden stops in the middle of nowhere.

Watch for unusual road signs; names of businesses; unique methods of advertising; types, quality and attitude of service; look for placards advertising special events or attractions you may not have included in your list.

When staying overnight, see if you notice anything special about the motel's service or facilities, its playground equipment; furnishings, advertising, etc.

Take a drive around town with an eye open for the new and unusual—or the old traditional symbols. Read the latest copy of the local newspaper . . . what problems are the residents coping with and how? You might find some answers to problems back home in their methods.

Once again, all of these things have story possibilities because America is a nation seeking answers to problems in cities and towns of all sizes. It's a nation of people on the go, with more time on their hands, seeking more places to visit—places besides the national monuments and traditional landmarks. This is where stories about places of interest just a few miles off the beaten path receive special consideration!

One thing about having the entire family along is that photographic models are never lacking! Most travel editors prefer people somewhere in a picture. We've got four at latest count in our family and can rotate personnel in various combinations of ages and faces . . . and have no problem obtaining model releases!

Does all this work? You bet it does! We've been doing it for years. Results have included a story and pictures to the *New York Times* travel section of a Canadian historical park, Fort Steele; a Y-Z (Yosemite to Zion) Trail article and pictures for *Westways;* a community project in which former government land was converted to a hospital and airport site at Canton, S.D. for *Empire Magazine;* skiing developments in the eastern Sierras of California for national skiing magazines; a story and pictures on the Madison Canyon Earthquake Area development as a tourist center for *Dodge News Magazine;* a visit with a man near Anaconda, Mont. who does antlercraft carving and horseshoe sculpture resulted in a story for *Grit.*

Others included a visit to a Bull Mountain ranch near Roundup, Mont. that resulted in a picture for *The Christian Science Monitor;* a radio telescope installation near Big Pine, Calif. provided copy for a feature in the *Monitor;* a silhouetted snapshot of two cowboys made a cover for a western magazine; a picture of an old mining camp with radar domes looming up over a distant hill made a cover for *Montana Parade.*

No doubt, by now you've seen the next step coming on how to make good things better. If these story possibilities exist in other towns you've visited, you've got all of them and even more right in your own back yard! You also have more time, personal knowledge and contacts from which to develop stories along the same lines.

Even weekend outings or Sunday drives lend themselves to the same treatment. Among local topics we've developed into stories in spare time have been multiple use of Flathead Indian

Reservation reservoirs for the *New York Times;* the Flathead Lake Showboat for *Grit;* an unusual newspaper ad for *Floor Covering Weekly;* the public relations policy followed by the local airport manager for *Air Facts;* a story on Pony Palace activities for various horse mangazines and a story on the Pony Palace community center for *Grit;* add to these scores of stories and pictures placed in regional newspapers and Sunday supplements.

If you like to visit certain places or are interested in a certain project or policy, it's a pretty good sign that other folks would find those same things interesting. The main thing to remember is that your copy-and-picture package must be slanted to fit the specific needs of the magazine or newspaper you're aiming for. If you can do that, you've made a sale.

Try it and see!

# Writing and Selling the Picture Book

## More than 1,000 children's books are published each year—why not yours?

*by Joan Potter Elwart*

Now LET'S SAY you've got a notebook full of ideas, and a whole afternoon to work. Where do you begin? I start with an eye on my market. Unless you write strictly for pleasure, you have to keep an eye on your editor. Reading through the juvenile magazine and book publishers sections of *Writer's Market* will give you a good idea of what editors want and don't want. Some stories are aesthetically acceptable, but simply don't fit into the image the editor has of his magazine or book list.

And notice I'm speaking of looking for magazine markets when our interest here is supposed to be books. The sad fact of publishing is that you very seldom can start at the top with a book. You have to prove you can sell to small markets and magazines usually, before a book editor is willing to gamble an enormous amount on your ability to please. So check your markets; magazines if you're a beginner; book markets if you've a few magazine credits under your belt.

The magazine markets are divided into two groups—the general interest magazines such as *Jack and Jill*, and *Humpty Dumpty*; and the religious markets. Sometimes the same story will not be acceptable in both markets, and you may have to make a choice. The religious markets often will not accept a story that only entertains; however, the general interest magazines will accept stories that illustrate a moral principle when the theme is subtly handled.

Notice the word limits, especially in those markets that you are particularly interested in. Few magazines use stories for young children that go over 1,000 words. Verse stories seldom are used, even if editors say they use them. Many magazines avoid fantasy, especially if it involves animating animals and objects. Stories told from a girl's point of view are hard to sell. Editors say girls can relate to a boy's point of view, but a boy won't identify with a girl's point of view. So your widest market would be for a story under a thousand words, about the real life adventures of a boy. I've sold more of this type of story than any other.

The book market is a little more elastic. Here editors are more open to fantasy and anything different. They can choose to aim for an all-girl market, so girls are more acceptable protagonists here. The story can also be much longer. Although, I think you need to take into consideration the fact that the attention span of the audience you are aiming at, the three to eight year olds, is only about ten minutes. Anything much longer than that and it's hard to hold their interest. Some editors feel, however, if they ask three or four dollars for a book, they have to give quantity to make the buyer feel he is getting his money's worth. For this reason, I think, there are many picture books on the market that are much too long. Quantity of enjoyment in books should be emphasized, rather than quantity of text.

Remember, too, that few if any book or magazine publishers permit fictional characters to do anything you wouldn't want the reader to imitate.

Now you've selected your material and word length with an eye on your market. If you're aiming at a magazine, your story has a better chance with a strong plot line. Books publishers are happy often with only a theme or an idea carried out as in *If Everybody Did.*

The standard definition of plotting is not valid for the below eight crowd—the one that says, a plot presents the protagonist with a conflict which he tries again and again and again to overcome, and finally *through his own efforts,* the protagonist's problem is resolved.

It is quite apparent that a young child is not in control of his life in the same way an adult is. So in a story for a young child, it is not always necessary for the child to solve his own problem. The solution may come from outside himself but, again, must be logical in terms of what has gone before.

Ludwig Bemelmans demonstrates an acceptable picture book resolution in his Caldecott Medal book *Madeline's Rescue* (Viking, 1953). Madeline's problem is two-fold: the school inspectors have chased away the children's dog; even with the dog in residence, the children are unhappy and fight because one dog is just not enough for twelve little girls. Madeline and her school friends tried but could not solve either problem; but the situation is resolved when ". . . suddenly there is enough hound to go all around," with Genevieve finding her own way back to school and then promptly presenting the girls with twelve pups.

In plotting and organizing a story, I make use of two mechanical devices. One is the refrain. This is a line usually repeated by the main character throughout the story. The gingerbread man that says, "Run . . . run, as fast as you can, you can't catch me, I'm the gingerbread man."

The other device is the use of a repetitious anecdote or theme, usually with a slight variation: Black Sambo meets three tigers in three anecdotes and deals with them in a way that varies only slightly from tiger to tiger.

After you've mapped out the plot and general structure of the story, again you make another choice; is this a story a child will read to himself, or is it for an older person to read to a small child? The easy-to-read story is in great demand, with fewer writers working in this area, but it is a difficult and challenging story to do. The writer is limited to the reading vocabulary of either a first or second grade child. Some publishers even restrict their authors to a particular word list; while others only insist that the words used in the story are either "sight" words taught to most six or seven years olds, or that the words can be attacked with the reading skills taught at this level. Unless the writer has a background in primary education, he will have to do some research in primary reading texts in order to write for these markets.

In the story to be read *to* a child, the writer has much more latitude in his choice of vocabulary, but he still is limited to what is easily understood by an eight-year-old at most. As a rule of thumb, a child should not be unfamiliar with more than one word in every three lines or he loses interest. The only way to find out, is to try your material out on children of the proper age.

Sentence construction should be quite simple. Listen to the natural speech patterns of children of this age to find the pattern they are most comfortable with. I find they seldom use anything but simple, declarative sentences in the active voice. They seem to find complex and compound sentences hard to follow. Faulknerian sentence structure is not for five-year-olds. The active voice gives any prose a feeling of immediacy, activity and sparkle. Using it is a good habit to cultivate in writing for any age.

A further examination of children's speech patterns will show that they depend primarily on nouns and verbs for expression and tend to ignore the use of adjectives or adverbs. Careful selection of nouns and verbs will make stories more colorful and direct. Watch the tense of verbs. The use of tenses that require the use of auxiliary verbs—am, will, had, was, etc.—tend to weaken the impact of sentences. Don't let the verb get too far away from its noun or you'll lose a child before he gets to the period.

Because children are especially delighted with music and rhythm, choose words that have these values. Alliteration, consonance, assonance, onomatopoeia, and cadence are the tools of the good juvenile author as well as the poet.

Now put these words together with a careful ear. Balance phrase against phrase, sentence against sentence. If you've done a good job on the story, the reader could no more leave out a word or phrase than he could in a poem.

One afternoon my daughter carried in Alvin Tresselt's *A Thousand Lights And Fireflies* (Parents' Magazine Press). My supper was cooking merrily on the stove, but we couldn't resist taking the time to sit down and try it out. As to be expected, it was so enjoyable my children insisted on another reading immediately. Listening to my supper bubbling away, I decided I had better condense. But every time I left something out, three-year-old Annie would stop me and say, "But, Mother, you didn't say . . ." and then quote the phrase or sentence exactly; and this after only a single reading.

So it's not only *what* you say in a picture book, but the way that you say it. For if all the writer has to offer is a plot, the young reader may as well restrict his reading to synopses of well-known books. The writer's burden then, and pleasure, is to show these little people that language itself has rhythm, color, harmony, music and fun.

Because these little children, in a sense are just coming alive, the information their sense brings to them is new, and fascinating with the attraction of the unfamiliar. Young children love to touch, smell, look, listen, taste—they savor and delight in these sensory impressions. So a picture book writer can add a new dimension of pleasure to a story if he can transmit these impressions to his reader. Don't just say something was good. Make the reader taste it. Don't just say it was noisy. Make him hear it.

As with good poetry, a good picture book should be emotionally evocative, leaving the reader with a feeling of triumph, or with any of the satisfying emotions.

One more thing a picture book writer must be alert to is picture possibilities of a story. A magazine may need to include only two or three situations that would lend themselves to illustration. But a picture book must be planned for from 15 to 30 pictures. Does your story have this many pictorial situations?

Now we've taken our idea—worked out the plot and design of the story—dressed it in rhythmical, musical prose. We've got our picture ideas in mind. Now we're off to market.

If you can illustrate the book, send samples, except where the publisher says not to. Check *Writer's Market* for editors' preference here.

However, Betty Ren Wright, Whitman's managing editor, stresses the fact that for her (and for most publishers too, I believe) it is not necessary to actually illustrate a picture book; a description of a picture is as acceptable as a sketch or photograph. She says, "Judging by the numbers of phone calls and letters we get, I think writers get hung up on this question very often and sometimes spend a great deal of money providing themselves with illustrations they consider passable."

Take time to check the physical makeup of the publisher you are aiming at, and fit your story into it. For instance, Whitman books usually have a line no longer than 36 characters long, seldom use more than ten lines to a page with a maximum of 125 lines to a book; 800 words is the usual overall limit—with a maximum of 32 pages, including cover. Actually making up a book for an editor makes life easier for her (she's better able to see the physical possibilities of the story) which in turn makes her more disposed to look on your submissions with approval. It also tells her you have an understanding of her problems—which, of course, is the mark of a professional.

When you don't make up a sample book, set up your manuscript the same as for any adult story. I sometimes leave a wide margin on the right and use the space to indicate verbally, in red type, accompanying picture ideas.

The make-up for an easy-to-read story, however, differs from the usual manuscript. At this age, the child is presented with few enjambed lines. Sentences should be completed on one line where possible. Each sentence is started on a new line. Paragraphing is indicated by triple spacing. Check primers at your library, if this make-up is hard to visualize. Include a vocabulary list with an easy-to-read story.

Then make up a list of ten or twelve markets and send it off to the first. Don't include a letter. Magazines answer in from two weeks to two months. Four or five months is not uncommon for a book publisher, so don't badger editors prematurely. When it comes back (they usually do, at least a few times), don't agonize; send it out to number two on your list.

Contrary to most advice, I do save quite a few rejection slips, as they often show a pattern. The first may be of the printed variety. The second may still be printed but may "welcome further submissions." Notes or letters, length of time held (when longer than usual for that particular publisher) all indicate special interest. You can see whether a particular editor likes your fantasy, an educational approach, or your easy-to-read story. Editorial responses can help you judge the value of a script, too; a writer is often his own worst judge.

Write regularly and get a backlog of different types of stories at the same age level. Keep hitting the same markets regularly. Even if you have no credits to indicate professionalism, your regular good submissions will tell the editor your work habits and attitudes are professional. He'll know you could rewrite if necessary to salvage a piece that just misses, and could repeat again and again for him if he gambles on publishing one of your stories.

Well, now the writer has his story in the mail he has time to think about the rewards he can expect from this business he has committed himself to. And, of course, we all anticipate a return for our efforts, either in terms of money or satisfaction or we just wouldn't be bothered. And there are rewards—but I think they are often grossly misrepresented.

Very few writers, I find, are able to earn their living solely with their picture books. The great financial successes, such as Dr. Seuss, are newsworthy because they are the exception. Still the opportunity is there.

One very successful book can be as good as an annuity. Munro Leaf says every night when he thanks God for the food on his table, he thanks Him also for Ferdinand who put it there.

While we all can't expect financial returns like this, the ordinary returns in terms of effort expended are usually quite good. One can expect a $500 advance plus 10% royalties from most publishers of picture books when you provide both illustrations and text. Half of this is the writer's if he provides text only.

Writing for young children, I've found, also has indirect rewards. As the previous material on the ingredients of a good picture book indicates and as any experienced juvenile writer knows, no other type of writing demands so much from the writer—a sharp mind, sharp senses, a keen ear and eye, and good judgment; therefore, no other type of writing can be quite as stimulating in terms of personal growth. Writing for young children does, indeed, prepare one for success in almost any other field of writing, for the simple truth is, after you've learned to write a good picture book, anything else is easy.

However, writing for children as well as being rewarding in terms of money and personal and professional growth, for me is just downright satisfying. I would rather win a Caldecott or Newberry medal for a child's book than a Pulitzer Prize. For the fact is, without people like us showing children the pleasure of good books, helping them form good literary attitudes and habits—there would never be a Pultizer Prize winner and no one to read or care about his books. And while this year's prize novel will wind up in next year's used book sale, I've never found a good picture book there yet. These are simply read and treasured till they fall apart. No other type of author has a more loyal audience. No other author is read over and over so many times and never forgotten.

And so when my little girl scrapes her knee and I sit her on my lap and when for the 100th time we turn that last page of our favorite book and she hugs herself with delight and says, "read it *again* . . .;" at these times I think to myself—this is the kind of immortality I'll settle for.

# Freelance Job Opportunity: Publicity Writing

**Nearly every youth, health or welfare agency in a fair-sized community needs part-time public relations help. Why not you?**

*by Patt Kirby McCauley*

MOST ASPIRING WRITERS, like anyone else, want to start—and stay—at the top. This is a neat trick. It has been done, but it's the exception rather than the rule.

If you seriously want to practice your craft and don't mind stepping on the first rung of the ladder, try turning your talents toward public relations work. It gives the writer practice, the satisfaction of seeing his work in print, and financial reward.

During the past 15 years, friends, neighbors and relatives keep asking me, "Just what *do you do?*" They know I write, keep mysterious hours and have an opportunity to meet many celebrities and travel. But the exact nature of my work is a complete mystery to most of my acquaintances.

Officially, according to the Internal Revenue Service, I am a Public Relations Consultant. Sounds pretty fancy, but it's a little better than flack, press agent or publicist. Actually getting down to cases, I do freelance publicity and public relations for anyone who wants to put their story in front of the public. The reason I don't classify myself as a publicist is because much of my work deals with radio and TV as well as printed materials.

I hope, eventually, to write the eternal book or receive regular assignemtns from the slicks. But till that time comes, I want to keep writing, learning more about people and their experiences and—make money. Even with my p.r. business going full tilt, six small children and an eleven-room house to keep in shape, I still manage some magazine sales.

Lets take a good look at the p.r. business. In most metropolitan areas, the field is a highly competitive one, but there's always room for a beginner with talent. Getting "in" is the first problem—staying there, the second.

Is there much money in p.r.? The only honest answer I can give is that the ceiling is almost limitless if you are honestly willing to work, and work hard. If a free-lancer would put full-time effort into his work, it is not inconceivable that he could easily make upwards of $24,000 every year.

Before you decide that the pasture looks pretty green, take a look at the bad side of the ledger. As a press agent you're neither fish nor fowl. You don't work for a newspaper, radio or TV station. Still, you're not an amateur tyro or a volunteer. If anything goes wrong—a candidate is defeated, a campaign fails to make it's goal or a show's "gate is down," *you're* the professional and it's always the fault of publicity!

Many newspaper reporters resent the p.r. specialist. They think you have all the free time in the world and make more money than the general assignment man. Sometimes this is true, but *you* take your job home with you—they don't.

If you have a thick hide, a good sense of humor and the constitution of a horse, go ahead. There's *money* in publicity.

Nearly every youth, health or welfare agency in a fair-sized community has or needs a part-time p.r. person. It is their job to handle news relations with all media and keep the organization's name in front of the public. Just check the yellow pages of your telephone directory under "organizations." There are dozens of them. Some will already have professional staffers, others will be working exclusively with volunteers. Be on the alert for up-coming fund-raising campaigns or local elections.

A newspaper background will be of tremendous help toward "getting in." You already know the value of a tight lead—how to cram the who, what, where and when into an interesting lead, and keep the why, in condensed copy. You'll know the value of *being accurate*. Heaven help the press agent who smokes up a story or plays with the facts. It's bad news. The editor will recognize it and you may as well go back to your mops and brushes.

For the writer without press experience, getting started will be a bit more difficult. First, study the newspapers in your area. Pay particular attention to the stories you would be likely to write as a p.r. person. One announcing a fund campaign, new officers or a service rendered by an agency. Pictures, though not a writer's field, are important. Think about ideas for eye-catching off-beat illustrations that will tell your story with just a legend caption. Don't forget features. These stories are important too, but most metropolitan papers assign features to one of their regular staff writers. The press agent, however, has to sell the editor on the idea, so be aware of slant, treatment and the kinds of stories that are used.

If a client wants a picture for the papers, it's up to you to set it up, make it interesting, and sell it to the press. The client pays for it. Most photographers charge a minimum of $10 to $20 for a picture set-up and one shot. Additional poses run about $5 each. If you just want to shoot exclusively for one paper, and you have a *news story plus good picture props,* call the newspaper's city desk and ask the city editor for a cameraman to shoot the picture. If you will be servicing more than one paper in the same area, engage your own photographer. Each picture should be different. Vary the people, set-ups and props. Giving the same picture to two metropolitan dailies is "the kiss of death." A city editor is not running a publicity circular for your benefit. The picture you offer him must be original and eye-catching.

In addition to organizations that might have need for a p.r. person, don't overlook special events that are coming to town. Political campaigns are also a good bet.

I've done work for Boy Scout Jamborees, dog, cat and horse shows, congressional and city council candidates and a host of health agencies. The list is endless of attractions and things that need news coverage.

If there is an auditorium or arena in your area where events are regularly held, check with the booking director to see what is scheduled. Work at least six months in advance.

Get the name of the person in charge of the event. If he is out of town, drop him a letter telling him you are interested in handling the publicity for his event. If you're a novice, think of some good ideas that might merit coverage for him. (Don't give them away in a letter—not everyone is as honest as you'd like to think.) Tell him you have some good promotional ideas you'd like to discuss with him. If you have newspaper experience, so much the better. Briefly outline your background for him.

Putting a price tag on your work is a difficult thing. Fees should be based on your experience and the time involved to complete the job. Most non-profit agencies will hire a part-time p.r. person on a monthly retainer basis. Determine with the agency executive or president, how much time you will have to spend on the job and if you are expected to cover special meetings. Make certain that this is determined in advance. You can run yourself ragged attending committee and board meetings, when just a simple glance at the minutes will give you all the material necessary for a follow-up story.

With special events and things of a "one-shot" nature, determine again, how much time you think the job will take. Then set a flat fee based on an hourly rate. How much are plumbers, carpenters and repairmen getting in your area? Isn't influencing public opinion just as important?

For a "one-shot" promotion, a show, political campaign or a special event, the usual rate (in the San Francisco Bay Area) is $20 per hour. Some clients prefer to work on an hourly basis, others on a flat fee. Your retainer should be determined by the number of hours you plan to spend on the job, and worked out to a flat fee. If you're engaged on an *annual* retainer basis and are paid *monthly*, the fee is usually discounted 10 percent.

Always be careful to find out about expenses. Mileage, postage, telephone and other items can mount up quickly. These should be billed to the client over and above your time for doing the job. If there is to be no extra allowance for expenses, make certain your fee is high enough to cover these things.

Any time you agree to do a "one-shot," have a written and signed contract. It can be very simple but *get it in writing*. It is also a good idea to request half the fee in advance.

## The Beginner

If you're a novice to newspapers, the best way to get started in publicity work is by offering to do volunteer work for someone. Although you won't get paid, the experience and contacts you will gain are worth more than money to the beginner. Most organizations are delighted to find a willing volunteer, and if you do a good job, you will be well rewarded in experience that will pay off in honest dollars in the months to come.

Developing a good relationship with the editor is very important. When you have your first story prepared, and your facts double checked, pay a personal call on the newspaper's city editor. Make your visit brief, but inquire about deadlines and the use of photos. Make it clear to him that you want to write copy that he needs and can use. Editors aren't ogres. They want to help you, but they don't have time to waste. As you become more familiar with the city room and its procedures, you'll know when it's the right time to stop and chat—or whether you should just drop your story and leave.

Always type and double space your copy. Put the name, address and telephone of the organization you represent, and your name and telephone number, in the upper left-hand corner.

Never write a headline. This marks you as an amateur. Newspapers have copy editors for that.

If, for some good reason, you want the story released on a specific day, indicate "for release—day of the week and the date" at the top of the page.

Keep it short. Most stories can be told in one page.

For non-profit agencies and fund-raising events for charity, don't overlook spot announcements for radio and television. The Federal Communications Commission requires that a certain amount of broadcasting time be given to public service, but the competition is keen.

Always make sure that any spot announcements are at the station an appropriate amount of time prior to the date you want them aired—public service announcements, ten days to two weeks; news items only three to five days in advance. Otherwise they get lost in the shuffle. Copy should be prepared in 10, 20, 30, and 60-second lengths. It's best to check with your local station to see which lengths they can best use. Spot announcements should be one to a page, typed double-spaced. Radio copy formerly was typed all caps (that's the way copy comes over the wire services), but more and more stations are using the more readable caps and lower case. The length of the spot should be underlined in the upper right-hand corner of each page. Spot writing is difficult. Sell your story without adjectives or lengthy prose. A 60-second spot runs 120 words; 30-second, 60 words; 20-second, 45 words; and the all important 10-second (especially for television), 20 words. The more copies you can send (no carbons or tissue sheets), the more chances for multiple exposure you have.

TV stations usually require a horizontal photograph to accompany all copy. (Some larger stations may already have 2x2 slides of important buildings, persons, in the community.)

In promoting your event, don't overlook spot news coverage or TV news features of the event in preparation. These have to be of exceptional quality, so really give this a great deal of thought before contacting your news director. The Public Service director of the TV station can be of help in placing your people on interview shows or arranging tapes to be played at various times throughout the day. If your event deals with sports, don't overlook all the sportscasters in your area.

As you become established, not only with the editor but within your community, as being a competent press agent, one that can turn out results and meet deadlines, jobs will come to you faster than you can handle them. Be careful though. Spreading yourself too thin can be a dangerous thing and result in a half-hearted job for all concerned. If you "goof" a story, not everyone is willing to give you a second chance.

Build your reputation and guard it carefully. Although you will rarely get a by-line for your work, you'll have the satisfaction of seeing almost every blessed line you'll ever write in print—and the compensation of getting paid for it too!

# Contests Pay Writers Two Ways

## The techniques that make you a consistent contest winner also help you with your other creative writing

### by Betty Stilwell Owens

WRITING A CONTEST entry is "fun" writing, but learning the techniques that make you a consistent winner also provides excellent groundwork for any type of creative writing you aspire to, whether stories, articles, or poems.

Give them half a chance and the raw psychology of contests will nab you. Here's an irresistible lure—a trip around the world, four years' college tuition for your child, $25,000 cash—and all for "25 words or less," the last line to a jingle, or for naming a race horse! Simple? And the possible rewards are terrific! Simultaneously, your interest and motivation are aroused, along with that touch of the gambler in you. Why not enter a contest? Anybody could do it. And so what if you lose? Very little time or money have been expended.

Contests are everywhere—in magazines, your newspaper, and in grocery store displays. Your eye lights on one that appeals to you, so you grab an entry blank, a pen, you write that entry and mail it. There, you didn't feel scared at all! You don't sit back and wait for the winners to be announced either. You enter another—and another. Now, if the first one doesn't win, you have the others to look forward to. And so it should be in your "real writing." You write one article, story, or poem, and immediately start on another.

Following the rules of the contest game, you've already adopted these valuable rules of the writing world: (a) you wrote it and mailed it (the deadline will get you if you don't watch out!); (b) you don't worry about the outcome of any particular piece, because (c) you've become productive. Right off, you conquer two common agonies of the would-be writer: the paralysis brought about by blank white paper, and the "shattering of the ego" experienced with rejection slips.

The basic requirements of a good contest entry are also the basic requirements for any good writing of a creative nature. As you proceed with our "fun" writing, you will be ingraining the disciplines you must master in becoming a "real" writer. It's a magical way to attain them, for the disciplines become second nature as you have so much fun you feel no pain at all!

*First,* you acquire a wide and colorful *vocabulary.* Duplication is the downfall of many a contest entry. Everyone says the same thing in the same old way, using the same bedraggled words and trite expressions we fall into using in our everyday speech. So, your search for THE word never ends. Finding one suitable word simply spurs you on to looking up all the synonyms in search of an even better word that is also apt, alliterative and a more striking way of expressing your thought. In a jingle contest, featuring Mrs. Filbert's Margarine, I borrowed words from another field altogether. The jingle went:

> Mrs. Filbert's Margarine
> Tastes so fresh and sweet
> For spreading and for cooking, too

In search of words that would be apt, colorful, and quite different from saying *the daily freshness was a great treat,* which was the *idea* I wanted to express, I used a newspaper analogy and said,

" 'DAILY NEW'S' A HEADLINE TREAT!" This won an electric range.

*Second, conciseness* is a *must.* "Wordiness" is a bugaboo every writer must fell before he can expect to become "salable." Contests have strict rules on wordage, and if the rules say "25 words or less," 26 won't do. You can write reams of deathless prose while developing a story or article; after all there's no editor standing over you with a sharp blade to chop out words and paragraphs at the proper times and places. But, if you aim to win that top prize you have your eye on, and the rules say "25 words," you'll comply. Since it's administered in small doses, a contest at a time, and say, cutting 50 words to 25, here again it's fun and painless. But you are becoming concise! Before you know it, you'll write a rough draft of an entry saying just what you want to say in the way you want to say it, you'll count the words, and guess what! It's exactly 25 words! In an Armour contest to tell "Where In the World I'd Like Most To Go and Why" it seemed sort of crazy to think you could tell them *where* you'd like to go in 25 words or less, much less *why*. Since my husband was stationed in Guam, this was my "place." Hitting on a familiar saying that "said a lot in a few words," my entry went: "Home is where the heart is— and I'd like to go 'home' to Guam—where *my* heart is."

This employed only 19 of the allotted 25 words and won a huge supply of food products. Conciseness becomes a challenge you can meet, and you'll find yourself plumbing the depths of your mind in quest of it, admittedly an excellent exercise for a writer, with all sorts of "fringe" benefits besides conciseness.

*Third, research* is absolutely necessary. As in other writing, where your instructors tell you to write about what you *know*, contests demand that you know what you are talking about. Even if it's only a cake of soap you're writing about, you must use the soap, compare it to others, study your sponsor's ads and claims as well as his competitors'. Only then will you *really* know why "I like Sudsy Soap *best* because . . ." Besides turning out to be fascinating little research projects, this area of contesting is extremely educational and will broaden your field of knowledge in ways valuable to your writing career. Delving into a particularly interesting subject may spark an idea for an article or story. You also find yourself increasingly *wanting* to know all about your subject, whether in contesting or other writing. Some of your earlier efforts, where you unashamedly wrote "off the top of your head," seem pretty shallow, even to you. It makes you blush to think how they appeared to an editor! In the Delco Battery Contest, my knowledge of batteries was less than nil, if that's possible. My total knowledge concerning a battery was that it would either make the car go, or it was "dead" and the car *wouldn't* go! Starting with batteries, period, I read all I could find on them, employing for my research the dictionary, encyclopedia, auto magazines, brochures about competitive batteries, and finally, "specializing" now on "my" battery, all the literature and ads available on the Delco Battery. If every natural-born enemy of anything mechanical became a convert, I did. A battery—that dread and secret source of my car's life—became something I could understand!

Boiled down to essence for contest purposes—the salient facts I needed to complete the Delco jingle were these: *Battery*—a device which generates electric *current* by transforming chemical energy into electrical energy. It consists of two or more electric cells which are joined together to provide a single source of electricity; *Ampere*—signifies the unit of *strength* or intensity of an electric *current; one of Delco's chief claims was the superior strength of their battery.* So familiar had I become with this battery-business, I even knew that amperes are affectionately referred to as "amps!" Here's the jingle, and note, especially, my last line:

> I like what Delco does for me
> Its year-round "start" security
> Saves me money, saves me time
> "World's champ" in "amps"—
> "beats" time and clime!

This won $100, or to satisfy the writer's scale of pay, $12.50 per word! But more than the momentary financial reward, the value of learning to love research is immeasurable to you as a writer. In this particular project, the word "ampere" so intrigued me that I tracked it down to its source, and found that it was named for the discoverer of its principle, French scientist Andre Marie Ampere. I found that all modern electric practice is based upon two simple laws, first stated by him. This fascinating man's theories that even I could understand, had their inception in the 1800's, and had lain dormant and neglected by me my whole life! I, who had always simply shuddered at electrical concepts, was led into pursuing a subject to the point where I could now write of it fairly intelligently if another piece of writing called for it. In fact, a recent experience growing directly out of this could provide the nucleus of a story. Driving merrily along in my car, it stopped dead in the middle of the street. Did I throw up my hands in despair and call a mechanic? No, I hopped out, threw up the hood, and found the *battery cable* had come loose. I jiggled it back into place and was on my way. How's that for a girl who didn't really know what a battery *was* before the Delco contest! I would say that a love of research is a prime requisite to become the writer you want to become. With your material grounded in facts, and with far more knowledge on a subject than you will actually use, word for word, you not only write fluently and tersely, but with an authority. What editor can long resist a writer like that?

*Fourth, explicitness,* or saying *exactly* what you want to convey, is another offshoot of contest writing that will carry over into your real writing. In a statement of 25 or 50 words, or a last line, there is no room for weak, ineffectual, or vague words. The best trick I know to develop this trait is to "sum up" a contest.

Decide what its *main theme* is, whether serious, clever, funny or tied into an advertising device the sponsor has chosen, such as a character or trademark associated with his product, or a season, Family Fun, or Vacation Time. Then, choose *THE important* feature or features of the product. Tie everything as directly as possible to what the sponsor and judges seem to want. Simply "get to the crux of the matter" and go on from there. I am sorry that the actual entry is restricted, but in a car jingle contest, my last line contained 5 words and won a $3,350 Dodge Lancer. You learn to make each word count, and with a background of research, vocabulary, and conciseness, you have all the elements necessary to "say *exactly* what you mean."

*Fifth, slanting* your entries to please the judging agency handling a particular contest is tantamount to pleasing the editor of a particular magazine. You know that you must study the magazine you wish to write for, to become cognizant of its type, "feel," and make-up, as well as the type of reader it is likely to attract. There are several judging agencies who judge most of the national contests. Some like meaty, apt, "plain jane" entries, other like clever, perky (though still apt) entries, some like a variety of "styles," and as you get further into the contest world you will see these preferences emerge. There are contest publications to keep you up to date on this and other "tricks of the trade," two of the best being *The Shepherd School* (their Contest Bulletin free by writing: P.O. Box 602, Willingboro, N.J. 08046) and *Jaybee's Contest Magazine* (35¢ from Box 39, Valley Park, Mo. 63088). The Mrs. Filbert's entry cited in this article was judged by Bruce, Richards (now D. L. Blair) who valued cleverness, rooted in aptness and originality. Chicago Donnelly judged the Armour Food Products entry on

the basis of aptness, originality, and sincerity. They also judged
the Delco Battery entry on the same basis, but you can see they
allow more leeway in originality, or a leaning toward cleverness.
It has been said that an amateur writer writes to please himself,
a professional writer writes to please others. Learning to please
the judges and the sponsor of a contest will teach you to look
and see what the other fellow wants before you begin to write,
and make you more concerned over what you are projecting to
your reader than just what you are getting off your chest.

*Sixth,* and surely the most fascinating facet of contesting
and creative writing in any field, is the brain-tingling fact that
you are dealing in *"ideas."* "What's the big *idea?"* is the question asked by contest judges and editors alike. The idea is what
you build an entry around and the idea is what determines a
winner. You build your story, article, or poem, on an *idea.*
Empty, beautiful, clever words strung together aren't in demand anywhere. My best ideas occur after the "spade-work"
is done. Steeping myself in the facts, via research, acquiring a
vocabulary apt to the subject, and then thoroughly reviewing
all of it, I then put it on a "back-burner" to simmer. No sweat
here. I take it out occasionally and mull it over, but I don't
force the actual writing. Then, boom! I get an idea. At this
point I do handsprings and grab a pencil. My labor has been
rewarded. I am ready to start writing. By this, I mean writing
the finished piece. I do much writing in the process of researching, and I believe actually writing it down helps to imprint it
on the mind and memory. At this point, where a good idea
comes, there is still work to do, but now I know where I am
going. From this point, it is truly fun, as the pieces fall into
place, and everything starts shaping up toward the realization
of the idea in all its fulfilled glory. This is what I consider my
"sure-fire" idea-getter. However, if you develop the habit of
keeping a keen mind, a sharp eye, and a "hearing" ear, ideas
abound in practically every situation and experience. Indulg-
ing in a bit of whimsy with my two youngest daughters produced an idea for a children's book soon to be published. Paula
and Sheryl had a miniature turtle. As we were leaving their
room to go swimming one hot summer day, we stopped a moment
to watch the baby turtle in his little pool. I said "Oh, don't
you know he would like to take off that hot shell and just

wear a swimsuit today?" The idea so delighted the little girls, I thought, "Wouldn't it be fun to see all the animals out of character and doing ridiculous things like that?" And so, *The Day the Zoo Went Cuckoo* was born. For a steady, sure output, however, such as a serious writer needs, I would say it is best to "dig" for your ideas. Latch on to unique, sound ideas when and where you may, but you can *create* them if you immerse yourself in your subject and then give it an opportunity to incubate. Your subconscious is your most precious ally.

# Over 100 Cash Markets Waiting: The Great Outdoors!

## How to get paid for enjoying yourself

*by Don Cullimore*

W HAT IS "outdoor writing?" What are the marketing opportunities? What are the primary areas in which a beginner would start? What articles sell, where do they sell, and how much is paid for them?

The average layman is inclined to think of an "outdoor writer" as one who gets paid for enjoying such recreation as hunting, fishing, boating and camping. To many a writing novice, the basic ingredient appears to be that of reporting a more or less memorable adventure in those realms of activity.

Fortunately, from an income standpoint, outdoor writing is neither that limited nor that simple. It offers opportunity for broad diversification in subject matter, treatment and marketing.

Beginning with the 1950s, outdoor recreation exploded into an all-family activity, diversified and extremely mobile. Boating and camping went into orbit, mostly family style. Hunting and fishing participation increased. Such allied activities as skin diving, water skiing, archery, skeet and trap shooting, handloading, backpacking and trail riding rose in popularity.

Interest in the conservation and esthetic aspects of the outdoors did likewise: Reclamation of despoiled lands and polluted waters; preservation of wilderness areas, wild rivers and scenic beauty; protection of endangered wildlife and vegetation (such as the whooping crane and redwoods); and nature appreciation in general are examples.

Outdoor recreational facilities proliferated—hunting and camping areas, launching ramps, docks and marinas, parks and preserves.

The outdoor product manufacturing field also mushroomed. New and improved types of equipment came in rapid succession, often made quickly obsolescent by additional refinements. (Consider the effect of the portable tent trailer on camping!)

The joint result of all these factors has been an almost incomprehensible expansion of marketing opportunities:

1. More periodicals with general interest in the outdoors.

2. More with a specialized interest—such as boating, camping, guns and hunting, conservation, etc.

3. More with a state or regional interest.

4. Other publications of a general or specialized nature (not normally of an outdoor type), seeking outdoor article material which (within their format) would fit their readership.

What is outdoor writing? As practiced today by the freelancer, it involves taking any facet of "outdoor interest" and converting it into material of appeal to a particular publication. No longer need he (or she) look primarily to "outdoor magazines"—they carry their subject matter into a multiplicity of periodicals.

## A Great Variety of Markets

The *Catholic Digest* carries an article on Sheldon Coleman's proposals for broad outdoor skill instruction in schools, with a sober appraisal of its sociological benefits in combating juvenile delinquency and improving the general physical fitness level. *Better Home and Gardens* publishes hints to the housewife on food planning and preparation in the cramped confinement of a small cabin boat. *Today's Health* takes a look at water skiing as a body builder. *Popular Science* analyzes new developments in snowmobiles—extensively used for hunting and ice fishing as well as for other transportation. In the house organ field, *Monsanto Magazine* discusses new plastic applications in pleasure boat construction. *The American City* reports on a municipality's achievement in civic marina construction.

There are four magazine category listings in *Writer's Market* which include a substantial number of publications with primary interest in outdoor material: "Sport and Outdoor Magazines"; "Travel, Trailer and Camping"; "Nature", Conservation, Ecology Magazines"; and "Regional Magazines".

Of the 100 or so "Sport and Outdoor" publications, 55 are

either primarily oriented, or specifically open, to outdoor material. In many others, in both this and other categories, the "outdoor angle" may be found which will fit their basic interest. (For example, a camping venture by bicycle or motorcycle could find acceptance in publications devoted to those subjects). Excluded from consideration are the definite sports-only (not outdoor) markets restricted to competitive athletics such as golf, bowling, football, basketball, etc.

The outdoor-oriented magazines can be generalized into eight categories:

1. *General outdoor magazines,* nationally circulated, such as the "Big Three" of *Sports Afield, Field and Stream,* and *Outdoor Life.* Hunting, fishing, camping and boating and all the allied activities and skills come within their scope. Conservation issues receive serious treatment. "How to" and "what to use" get detailed attention. "Where to go" and personal experience articles are sought—the two often being combined.

2. *Regional outdoor magazines.* Some are private (not state) publications, such as *Alaska Sportsman, Western Outdoors,* and *Southern Outdoors.* Content of the private publications largely parallels the "Big Three" with, of course, regional restriction. State agency publications vary in policy; usually place heavier emphasis on conservation information than "where to" and "how."

3. *Guns and hunting magazines.* Most include a combination of technical firearm material, "how to," hunting articles, tournament reports and gun collector hobbyist material. *Guns and Hunting* and *Shooting Times* are examples. Among the specialized are *American Field* (dogs), and *The Handloader.*

4. *Camping and trailering magazines.* Two types: General camping magazines (*Better Camping, Camping Guide*) which deal with tent camping as well as travel trailers and truck campers; and the trailering publications which are restricted to material relating to those recreational vehicles (*Trailering Guide, Trailer Travel, Wheels Afield,* etc.). These are not primarily interested in fishing and hunting—but will accept coverage of such as a phase of camping and trailering life. Travel gets much emphasis, but must relate to the experiences and advantages derived from camping and recreational vehicle usuage. "What's new," "how to" and technical information extensively used.

5. *Boating magazines.* In general, these not only cover the

"where," "how," equipment and venture aspects of boating, but range broadly into aquatic activities (racing, skin diving, water skiing). Much technical material is carried, relating to the extremely varied types of equipment, gear and skills involved in this versatile field. Emphasis varies; *Yachting* and *Motor Boating*, for example, lean more heavily to the big-water craft than does *Boating*.

6. *Fishing magazines.* There are many small regional publications in the sport fishing field, particularly in coastal areas. The three major ones are *Sportfishing*, *Fishing World* and *Salt Water Sportsman*. Coverage includes equipment, techniques, experiences, "where to," conservation problems, etc.

7. *Archery magazines.* This is the only one of the eight "outdoor" categories in which this writer has never marketed. I know of only two, *Archery World* and *Bow and Arrow*. Interests include both field archery and bow hunting, field experiences, "where to," tournaments and technical subjects.

8. *Conservation magazines.* Quite a few come in this category insofar as content may be allied one way or another with conservation. *National Parks, National Wildlife, American Forests, Sea Frontier, Audubon,* etc., are listed under "Nature" magazines. Many other conservation-minded publications are found in the "Sport and Outdoor" and "Regional" listings. Each must be studied separately, no generalization can be made.

In subject matter the field's expanding; outdoor writers in the northern U. S. and Canada have embraced snow-mobiling as a topic.

Travel or outdoor story? Travel is indigenous to the outdoors, and the outdoors is indigenous to virtually all travel articles which touch on the "open spaces." *Motor News* (Michigan) is typical of many in the regional/travel field . . . "interested in things to do—subjects concerning boating, fishing, hunting, camping. . . ."

Among "company publications" are many opportunities: *Outdoors,* external house organ of Kiekhaefer-Mercury (motors), concentrates on "where to go," facilities, and interesting exploits involving boating. *Ford Times* and Chevrolet's *Friends* carry travel articles which may include the outdoor aspect.

And there are trade magazines impinging on the outdoor scene: *The Boating Industry, Fishing Tackle Trade News, Sports Age, The Shooting Industry,* in the market for articles on merchandising of outdoor equipment. Rates are usually modest, but it's a good side market for material that can be picked up in the normal course of gathering outdoor information.

## Ideas Are All Around You

If by this time you suspect I am advising the beginner in the field to look almost anywhere for marketing opportunity—you're right. Study each section of *Writer's Market*, item by item, jot down notes . . . (as I've been doing). Search for subjects that will fit a special-interest category. It just occurred to me that I know of an outdoor-skill local program for youth, conducted by a civic club, that's a "natural" for the club's national publication (Association, Club and Fraternal Magazines). And I'm kicking myself for not having realized that the Canadian bush pilot I flew with last summer, who had participated in unusual fly-in wildlife study and rescue work in the roadless North, would have been an excellent subject for *The Cessna Pennant* (Company Publications).

Nor does the list of potentials end with *Writer's Market* listings. There are many relatively small regional publications, some of the magazine and some of tabloid newspaper format, dealing with one or more phases of the outdoors that you'll see on your local newsstands or in outdoor equipment stores.

There are also various hunting, fishing, boating and general outdoor "annuals." (Some are published by industry, such as the *Garcia Fishing Annual*). Outdoor books are appearing by the dozens, ranging from pocket-size how-to softbacks up to $15.95 "coffee table" volumes with elaborate color plates.

## What About Newspapers?

Newspaper coverage of the outdoors has been steadily increasing, and the weeklies and smaller dailies in particular may afford an opportunity for the writing aspirant to acquire background and experience.

Most frequently, coverage on papers of less than 50,000 circulation is handled part-time; either by a staffer assigned to other news duties, or by a freelance contract writer paid on a per-column or space basis. Many have never instituted consistent coverage.

Even the larger papers can often use on-the-spot reporting of special events, and outdoor-type features from free-lancers.

*Tips:* Check with sportsman and boating clubs, conservation agencies and personnel, and other sources of information. Keep an eye out for new facilities, "where to" locales, unusual hunting and fishing experiences, contests (such as field archery meet or field trial), exhibitions, etc.,—any "spot news" or features involving outdoor activity, conservation programs or conflicts. Come up with ideas that can fill a void in coverage by newspapers in your area. With written samples, you may be able to sell the editor on "stringer" coverage—and possibly a regular column.

### How's the Pay?

Due to the broad range of magazines and the variations in policy, only a general statement can be made as to rates. In the outdoor field itself, they run from the "acceptable" down to the ridiculously low. Some pay on a per-word basis; others on a flat-rate range within circumscribed article lengths. Some have specific separate rates for photos, but the prevailing tendency is to purchase photos and manuscripts as a "package."

In the "Big Three" general outdoor magazines, payment runs from about 10 cents a word up, depending on assignment and with variances based on photography, writer time and research in obtaining material, and other factors. Black and white photos go in the range of $25 each, color at $50.

Regional outdoor magazines vary from one cent to six cents per word, with lower rates generally paid by the state agency publications. Guns and hunting magazines range from four cents to six cents a word; camping and trailering from two cents to ten cents; boating and fishing magazines from four to ten cents. Quoted archery magazine rates are $75 to $100 tops for a full-length piece (1,000-2,500 words).

Comparable variations—from one cent to ten cents plus— are found in all other magazine categories in which openings exist for outdoor material. Beginners usually get the near-minimum of a publication's stated rates; a "name" writer may exceed the quoted maximum.

## How To Get Started

For the beginning outdoor writer, I would suggest studying the geographical area with which he (or she) is familiar to ascertain what's there, or what is happening, that conceivably could be developed in an "outdoor" article. Then study magazines selected for their potential interest in that type of subject. Regional and specialized smaller magazines, particularly those with a "where to go" slant, frequently offer the opening wedge.

In making this study, (and subsequently), compile ideas in the six major areas of outdoor writing:

1. "Where to go," with descriptive material on the geographical setting, perhaps a touch of history and lore; and outdoor offerings in terms of hunting, fishing, boating, camping and other attractions. Gather detailed information on facilities—camping areas, access points, marinas, guides, accommodations, etc.

2. Personal venture-type articles, describing a trip or experience. The routine "me and Joe went fishing" is largely "out" —unless it has an angle that lifts it out of the ordinary. Editors are on the lookout for articles on new and little-known locales; particularly if they're also descriptive of an unusual venture— *plus* adequate details on facilities.

3. Controversial subjects involving natural resources; such as the damming of rivers, pollution, fish and game laws, wilderness area and wild river preservation, game range destruction, etc. Also, legislative or administrative acts affecting outdoor recreation.

4. Organized activities, such as boat cruises, trap and skeet contests, field trials, archery meets, etc.

5. The "how to" or any of the multitude of skills involved in outdoor recreation, or of any one phase of those skills. "How to fish for Lake Michigan coho," for example, would deal with equipment, rigging and techniques. A "how" can describe the installation, use and maintenance of any equipment item related to the outdoors; advise on canoeing a whitewater river, or delineate standards in selecting a deer gun. It opens a broad range for imaginative development.

6. "What's new" in equipment. Outdoor recreationists are largely hobbyists—and most magazines in the basic outdoor

field cater to this with descriptive roundup articles and field report sections.

Points 5 and 6 may lead you into the "expert" or "specialist" field in some particular phase or phases of the outdoors; which can be most remunerative if you attain general recognition therefor. Magazines seek by-line specialists known to their readership.

Combined with your study of the magazines (their subject matter, style, requirements and needs), you now have the pieces to complete your outdoor writing jig-saw puzzle. Take any of the ideas under the eight points above, or combinations thereof, and see what fits the requirements and format of which magazine. It's strictly a matter of analysis.

In addition to the ability to write acceptable copy, two ingredients are essential to success in this field:

1. Photography—*quality* photography, in concept, composition, tonal contrast and illustrative relationship to the text. Today's editor looks first at the photos, loses interest rapidly if they're inadequate. Admonitions: Plan your basic pictures in advance and concentrate on them. You can always fill textual deficiencies by research—but you can't compensate for a missing key photo. Where the article's descriptive of an area, be sure and obtain a "mood" shot, such as a scenic that characterizes the geographical setting.

2. Adequate technical knowledge for descriptive accuracy in anything involved—whether it be equipment, skills, methods, fish and game habitat and habits, geography, facilities or whatever. You're writing (and photographing) for a critical audience that will gleefully seize upon any slip for a caustic letter to the editor! If you don't know—research!

For the career freelancer, outdoor writing requires a substantial time investment in travel, background research, market study and nose-to-the-grindstone writing. Field work can be fun or frustrating; weather can hopelessly foul up needed photography, fish and game may not cooperate. Financial returns are from low to moderate.

On the other side of the coin, it means a gratifying amount of active outdoor life, a continuous kaleidoscope of interesting places and people, and a wide range of information that a skillful "pro" can use and re-use to fit the needs of varied markets.

Once established in the field, I doubt if a writer would trade it for any other career—I know I wouldn't!

## Outdoor Writers Association

The versatility of outdoor writers is evidenced in a recent survey of the 1,400 members of the Outdoor Writers Association of America.

More than 50 percent are combination writer/photographer.

Fifty-six percent are active in more than one media; in various combinations involving newspapers, magazines, books, radio, TV, and motion pictures.

Fifty-five percent write for newspapers; 23 percent have magazine staff affiliation, and 43 percent freelance to magazines. Fifteen percent engage in radio, 15 percent in television, and 17 percent have authored one or more books.

Twenty-four percent are engaged part-time in lecturing or other public speaking, usually with their own color slides or film. Eighteen percent implement their income with sideline public relations and marketing consultant work. (These figures reflect many duplications; some are active in as many as five media fields).

The association was founded in 1927 and its headquarters are in the Outdoors Building, Columbus, Mo. 65201. Dues are $15 per year with an initiation fee of $5.00. It publishes a paperback, *Outdoor Writers Instruction Manual* (3.00), which can be ordered though *Writer's Digest*.

# Sell Photo-Illustrated Articles

## And get two checks instead of one

*by Arvel Ahlers*

WE WATCHED PETE from the shadows of the old United Nations Building at the World's Fair grounds in Flushing Meadows, Long Island. He was 14 years old, my youngest student in the photojournalism class. His father, a newspaper columnist, had tipped me off that Pete meant to do a series of illustrated "pieces" on "The Birth Of A World's Fair." Pete had no idea we were there to see how he'd go about it.

He began with a construction foreman near the base of the huge Unisphere. We saw him take notes on details the foreman pointed out, then sidle up to a group of workmen. Presently he unslung a camera and took a few snapshots. Moments later he vanished into the cloud of yellow dust being raised by the bulldozers along the promenade mall.

"He's going at it like an old pro," I said.

His father's eyes glinted. "I'll buy you a drink," he said.

The outcome of Pete's venture? His pictures turned out to be mediocre technically—but he had filled his negative area (2¼-inches square) with interesting subject matter. Out of about 60 exposures, he had 8x10-inch semi-glossy prints enlarged from 15 negatives. His text and captions required another trip back to the Fair grounds to pick up salient facts—including the *proper* spelling of names, titles and products involved. Eventually, though, this has been the return on his work to date:

a) $15 for text and 2 pictures bought by an architectural trade journal.

b) $18 for 3 heavily captioned pictures to be used in a concrete manufacturer's house organ.

c) A request for 3 new pictures and 500 words of text for which a steel manufacturer paid $50.

d) Two requests for short text-and-picture coverage of specific exhibit buildings.

e) Queries from newspaper Sunday supplements in Amster-
dam and Berlin where duplicate copies of 1,000 word articles and 6 pictures eventually sold.

Not a bad take for a kid of 14, would you say? Pete's experience underlines two significant points: 1) Each sale (and new
request) hinged upon a *combination* of text and pictures. 2)
*Multiple* sales of the *same basic ingredients* more than made up
for small individual sales.

Today, Pete is a full time professional freelance photographer
—and he follows exactly the same marketing techniques he
used in selling World's Fair pictures with text.

In my opinion, every writer of nonfiction should explore the
matter of using pictures to help "clinch" the salability of his
text. While there is no substitute for good, solid prose, pictures
can definitely provide the extra fillip that causes an editor to
reach for a check requisition instead of a rejection slip.

I discovered what pictures could do for my nonfiction sales
when a snapshot I'd been referring to for a "build-it-yourself"
article inadvertently went to market with my manuscript. An
editor's check for the text *plus $1 for the picture* completely al-
tered my writing career. After four out of my next six picture-
bearing "test" submissions drew checks, I invested $75 in a new
camera—and 35¢ in a book on picture-taking. It was the best
investment I ever made.

For the past two decades, about 70 per cent of my output in
books, customer-oriented product and service booklets, company
sales promotion manuals, etc., have been photo-illustrated. None
of my pictures rise above the "functional" level. Their purpose
is simply to clarify the text and/or lend eye-appeal to the
printed page. If circumstances are such that I can't shoot my
own pictures for an article or book, I get them from other
sources. That's the beauty of the whole thing—the alternatives
a writer has to choose among in getting the pictures he needs.
Let's talk about those alternatives.

## If You Shoot Them Yourself

This isn't the place to go into detail about camera equipment.
Essentially, you need a camera which, at the very least, lets

you adjust the lens focus for close-ups, medium distance and faraway subjects. Cameras that provide these minimal lens settings (often referred to as "zone focusing" adjustments) are available to accommodate several different sizes of film.

An editor doesn't care what size of negative a black-and-white picture is enlarged from so long as the final result features sharp images and good reproduction quality. If you intend to take *only* black-and-white pictures, therefore, the economy, compactness and dollar-value versatility of a 35mm camera may appeal to you.

If you expect to take color pictures, however, your best bet is a camera which yields *transparencies* no smaller than 2¼ inches square. For many years the amateur and professional choice in this size has been a single-lens or twin-lens "reflex" type camera. The viewfinder of a reflex camera lets you preview the images of your subject in the exact size and relationship they will be recorded in a negative or color transparency.

The most inexpensive way to produce enlargements to accompany your manuscripts (in the long run) is by doing all your own black-and-white developing and printing. In time you may come to this, as I did, but in the beginning you'll be better off if you let a custom lab or an advanced amateur darkroom enthusiast handle your negative and print developing problems. A custom lab (listed as such in a metropolitan classified phone directory under "Photo Finishing") will charge a fee for developing your film by hand. For another fee of $1.00 or thereabouts, the lab will make a sheet of "contact proofs" of the negatives you've exposed on a roll of film. The contact sheet provides "positive" images for study purposes—each picture being the exact size of the negative that recorded it. The pictures you select can then be enlarged to 8x10 inches. Most custom labs charge $1.50 per print, give or take 50¢. Smaller prints, of course, are somewhat cheaper; larger prints come higher.

## If You Team Up With A Photographer . . .

Many writers simply don't want to bother with a camera. They prefer to have a photographer handle all aspects of picture production.

This involves a fee problem which is generally solved in one of three ways:

a) The writer pays a flat fee for the photographer's time, materials, expenses, etc., *plus* an additional sum for *each* negative he wants prints made from. Sometimes the writer becomes sole owner of the selected negatives, in which case he is entitled to all income derived from them. More often, the writer pays a smaller fee per print and the photographer retains title to the negatives with or without the option of trying to market prints made from them himself. As you can see, there are all sorts of details involved. That is why there is no standard price scale applicable to this type of arrangement. A working plan agreeable to both parties has to be evolved from discussion.

b) For obvious reasons, most writers prefer to team up with a photographer (often a competent advanced amateur) who is willing to work on a percentage basis. Some teams operate on the "to each his own" principle with each partner receiving whatever a buyer has paid for the text and picture portions respectively.

A more popular working arrangement follows these lines: when a job is completed, the writer and photographer itemize their expenses (excluding time, of course,) on the index file card that will control the article's market routing. If the article sells, all expenses come out of the check first. The balalnce is then divided 50-50.

Different situations call for different working arrangements. The important thing for a writer and photographer to arrive at is a complete and thorough understanding of their working arrangements *before* they tackle their first job together.

## Outside Picture Sources

Quite often a writer isn't in a position to obtain on-the-spot pictures of a given locale, subject or product. In this case, he can always solicit illustrations from the photo libraries that maintain literally hundreds-of-thousands of pictures for editorial use. These libraries provide pictures either free or at low cost; don't confuse them with photo agencies which, although a picture source to keep in mind, charge from $10 or $15 up to several hundred dollars for "one-time publication rights" to their pictures.

Since an excellent compilation of free and low cost picture sources appeared in the 1968 *Writer's Yearbook*, available at your library, I won't repeat the sources here. Instead, I'll comment on a few additional places where free or low cost pictures are available.

Most cities have a Public Relations Department which maintains pictures of prominent buildings, streets, landmarks and cultural, recreational and civic scenes. They also include pictures of special events such as fairs, rodeos, annual parades, regattas, important sporting events, tourist attractions and the like. Selections of these pictures are often available by simply describing your needs and the use the pictures will be put to in a letter addressed to the city's "Public Relations Department."

When your article relates to the specific products of a major company, you can often obtain illustrations by either writing to the public relations department of the company itself, or to the advertising agency that handles the company's account— whichever is most convenient. By either route your query will usually wind up in the right hands.

In addition to federal picture sources such as the Library of Congress and National Archives, all states and territories maintain local "Travel Information Officers." The correct names and addresses of these offices are available from your local library. As we mentioned before, pictures from these sources are either free or provided at a cost of about $1.00 per 8x10 enlargement.

## Do's and Don'ts in Submitting Pictures

Every rule has its exception. The following rules, however, reflect what I've learned in marketing my own text-photo material—as well as that of other writer-photographers—internationally over a period of many years.

1. Do stick close to the standard 8x10-inch format (glossy or semi-glossy) in your black-and-white prints. Caption each print fully and factually with information that *supplements* (rather than repeats) your article text.

2. Do provide color *transparencies* (when needed) no smal-

ler than 2¼-inch square in size. Very few American or overseas editors will even consider 35mm color. The few who do accept this size are overwhelmed with competitive offerings.

3. *Don't* submit sepia toned or hand-colored black-and-white prints. Protect your prints with flat pieces of cardboard; never use mailing tubes.

4. *Don't* submit color *prints.* If you have any question about the difference between color *prints* and color *transparencies,* have your photo dealer explain the difference before you buy a roll of color film.

## Vive la Parlay!

Think in terms of multiple, non-competitive markets for your text-and-photo contributions *before* you tackle a subject. Think, too, in terms of different ways in which to present your basic material; i.e., feature articles, picture-sequence stories, fillers, and potboilers. Here, for example, is a true case history of the way in which a free-lance writer-photographer has "parlayed" her sales internationally:

Rosemary Beck, a California housewife, dreamed up gag lines to go with situations involving the postures and expressions of her three basset dogs. Despairing of having professional photographers capture the poses she wanted, she bought a camera and learned to use it herelf. Since then, her hilariously captioned pictures have appeared in LIFE, several newspaper Sunday supplement sections, and on several sets of greeting cards. Simultaneously, many of the *same* pictures with different story-telling captions and anecdotes have been published in Britain and France. Someday she plans to bring out books built around the tried-and-true material she has parlayed internationally.

## Other Markets Galore

There are estimated to be 10,000 house organ publications in North America and at least that many again in Europe and the Commonwealth. The bulk of these publications are wide open for free-lance text-and-picture contributions tailored to their specific needs. In countless instances the same *basic* material can be reslanted to meet the needs of non-competitive house organs, trade journals, non-newsstand circulated magazines, local newspapers and the like.

Along altogether different lines, there is a constant demand for photo-illustrated books of all types. Some publishers are producing juvenile, how-to-do-it, travel, hobby and recreational books by hiring writer-photographers on the conventional "advance plus royalty" basis. A growing trend, however, is toward "company-sponsored" books (and booklets) either contracted for by the company itself, or produced as a subsidized book by an established publisher. Either proposition is music to the ears of the free-lance writer-photographer. It means a guaranteed return—usually a fat basic fee plus royalties.

I'm frequently asked how many *different* markets exist for text-with-photo material. That's like asking how many stars one can see in the sky. It's a question of magnitude. On a clear night, with an unobstructed view, about 7,000 stars are visible to the naked eye. Similarly, it's no trick at all to see 7,000 different markets. The trick is to try to count the different stars—*or markets*—when you begin to view them through a telescope!

# How to Sell a Syndicated Newspaper Column

## Tips from a husband-wife team which does it.

### by George and Katy Abraham

A WHIMSICAL EDITOR ONCE said that the odds against giving birth to triplets are 6,400 to 1, and the odds against giving birth to a self-syndicated column are even greater. Is it possible to self-syndicate your own column? We asked this question to editors 22 years ago, after World War II, when we decided to swap our trigger finger for a green thumb.

"The Green Thumb" was the title of a column I dreamed about way back in the North African invasion when I was a soldier. I envisioned an indoor and outdoor gardening column that would help Americans grow better lawns, shrubs, fruits, flowers and vegetables. Editors told me later that it was practically impossible to launch a self-syndicated feature because they are daily being bombarded with "all kinds of stuff" some written by big name people. How could they afford to try something written by an unknown who had only a neat little title?

"I'm not taking 'No' for an answer" I told my wife Katy. With 40 million gardeners in America, there must be a need for a good garden column. People need help and advice on gardening matters, just as they do on food, sex, or managing a home. We were graduates of Cornell University, owned a small-town greenhouse and landscape business, and thought we were qualified to help people with gardening problems.

"Grass roots advice, that's what people want," Katy said. So we decided to launch "The Green Thumb," a down-to-earth advice column which plant growers could use.

Since you can always learn from someone else's mistakes, we want to point out some helpful tips we stumbled across during the period we built up our Green Thumb feature, and gladly share them with you. Our feature appears in 130 newspapers throughout America, with 5 million readership. Every reader of this book has the same opportunity to write, as a sideline or to make it a full-time business. Some of the things we found out the hard way are so simple we often wonder why they weren't taught to us in the eighth grade. Here they are:

1. *Have a Good Letterhead!* You've got a selling job to do and you can't sell with a sloppy or cheap letterhead. Don't be afraid to spend $100 to have designed and printed a simple, yet attractive letterhead. Editors can't see you in person (in my case it was a good thing because I wouldn't win any prize for good looks). Have envelopes made up also. Our slogan "The Green Thumb is *Read* All Over" appears on both our letterhead and envelope.

2. *Learn How To Write a Good Letter!* Our formula for writing letters (and our column) is "Short and Sweet . . . and Full of Meat!" Address your letter to a person, not just "to the editor" or "To Whom It May Concern," or to the Publisher. Letters addressed to nobody are food for the waste basket. (*The Editor and Publisher Yearbook*, 850 Third Ave., New York, N.Y., lists newspaper editors' names and addresses. It sells for $10.00—Ed.) Longwinded letters suffer the same fate. When writing to an editor, the No. 1 job is to tell how you can *help* his readers get more out of his paper. The reader is the backbone of a paper and they are everybody's bread and butter. If you have something different, tell the editor in as few words as possible.

3. *Don't Be Afraid to Work on a Good Letter!* Let someone else read it when you've cooked it up. For example, my wife and I spent two weeks polishing, writing and rewriting a letter to the editor of the nearby *Buffalo Courier Express*. He wrote back to tell us he was keeping our letter on file. We had our toe inside his door! When we did not hear from him, we wrote another letter two weeks later, and spent three days polishing up that epistle. We landed the Buffalo paper, our first big daily, on the strength of a well concocted letter.

Letters should be warm, neatly typed (no misspelled words or strikeovers!). Never send out form letters. This is really a waste of time for anyone who wants to reach a newspaper editor. If you send reprints (discussed later), manuscripts or any material you want returned,

4. *Always Enclose a Self-Addressed Stamped Envelope.* If you don't, kiss your material goodbye forever, because editors are swamped with scads of releases and promotional material. We *always* enclose a self-addressed, postal card for return, when feeling out an editor. All he has to do is check it and mail it. Here's what we put on our postal cards:

> Dear Green Thumb:
> Send us more information————————
> Send us samples————
> Send us column————
> Send us promotion————
> Send us rates————
> Send us your regards————
> COMMENTS:
> > Sincerely,
> > Editor
> > City————————State————————

A card like this, sent along with your letter, makes a contact which we follow immediately with information needed. Most editors don't like to throw away a five-cent card, even if it doesn't come out of pocket, so they are inclined to fill it out and mail it back to you. He may not buy it, but you've made contact. Notice, we did not leave a NO space. Why put negative ideas in an editor's mind? If he has a choice between Yes and No, he might select No. A self-addressed card like this is all the more reason why you should address your letter to a person.

5. *Start Out Small:* Don't try to land a big daily the first thing. An editor would be crazy to take on an unborn and untried feature. Whenever we speak to a journalism class about this, their first question is: "How can we get started if we don't ask editors to buy our work?" This is a good question. My point is that you have to start *small!* Write for a weekly, even if you only charge $1.00 a week. Get an article with your name on it. Then have reprints made and use these for ammunition for approaching editors. When you write an editor, enclose a reprint, along with your self-addressed, five-cent postal card. We started with weeklies at $1.00 per week then hit the dailies

where we charge according to their circulation. (Some rough guidelines: a weekly newspaper, with under 20,000 circulation, might pay $1.00 for a weekly column; a daily of 100,000, $5.00 for a weekly column; and a very large circulation daily, $25.00.)

6. *Reprints Tell a Big Story:* You may think reprints of an article cost a lot of money. They're worth every penny you spend. Reprints are a lever which helps you get your toe inside a newspaper's door. Put a little extra dressing on top to let the busy editor know what it's about.

Some of our reprints have this message on top:

> "Mr. Editor . . . here's why *The Green Thumb Is Read All Over.* Newspaper editors like yourself prefer "The Green Thumb" because it's Up-to-Date and Down-to-Earth . . . just right for busy readers who want a Green Thumb without an aching back.
> Gardening is America's No. 1 hobby.
> Why not try "The Green Thumb"—free for three weeks—so your readers can pass judgment on us firsthand?"

7. *Have Something To Sell!* This probably should head the list, because if you don't have a good service to sell an editor, better not try. If we didn't provide a service to the editor and to his readers, The Green Thumb would wither on the vine. It takes hard work to self-syndicate and it takes even more work to keep what you've gained.

8. *Don't Be Impatient!* Most people who write have a collection of "Sorry but we're keeping your letter on file . . . just in case the space situation gets better" (space referring to space in paper). A lack of space is the most common reason editors give us for not taking on The Green Thumb. *Don't be impatient.* It took us 22 years to land 130 papers, and if I didn't have an understanding wife, I'd probably have given up when our weekly take was only $5.00 the first year we wrote. One thing leads to another, like a chain reaction. Editors study features and they often ask one another about certain types at conventions. We're grateful for the help editors have given us by telling others about our feature. I now have many editor friends whom I may ask to write a letter of recommendation to a "hot" prospect. It all takes time and hard work.

9. *Be Promotion Minded.* Big syndicates promote themselves

by advertising and by agents who travel from city to city. We promoted ourselves every chance we had. When the *Saturday Evening Post,* a number of years ago, did a 10,000 word color story on our green thumb enterprise, we capitalized on this by sending a release to editors, along with a reprint. When the National Garden Bureau and American Seed Trade Association cited us for outstanding gardening journalism in America we took advantage of this and sent out a release to our papers, along with a mat showing Katy and me working in our greenhouse.

Another way we promote ourselves is to send testimonials—good letters from readers—to editors. Editors like glowing letters from readers and we make it a point to get them to the boss. Sometimes a reader is so thankful when we bend over backwards to supply him with an answer to a personal question on gardening, he asks if he can do anything in return. We say yes, write and tell your editor you like our service. It's a strange thing but most readers never think about writing a kind word, and it doesn't do a bit of harm to drop a gentle hint.

10. *Be An Expert:* The field you're contemplating should be one you know from A to Z. You won't know all the answers, but you should set yourself up as an expert, and here's the hard part: *Invite queries!* Fan mail is the yardstick editors use to measure the value of a new feature. This isn't always true since many "big name" writers never pull enough mail to fill a mosquito's eye. We invite queries and offer bulletins (free of charge) to attract mail. Some papers send us fan mail wrapped in shoe boxes, and it takes some doing to process this volume of letters. When our kids were home we had a nightly mail sorting bee, now I'm fortunate in having my aunt help us with the processing of mail. Most editors keep a mail count and some proudly boast that our take is greater than *Dear Abby's.* Another advantage of mail: it gives us some idea what's bugging people and it also gives us some good tips to use for the column. We'd grow stale if it were not for mail. And I might add here, when you give out advice, keep it simple. Our style is geared to an eighth grader—probably because we aren't smart enough to be a fancy writer!

And here's an ace up our sleeve: free bulletins or leaflets. We have over 300 different titles, ranging from *How To Lick a*

*Mole* (garden variety) to *How To Grow Nuts in Your Back-yard* (sometimes it's easy to go nuts!). These leaflets serve two purposes: they give readers information for their green thumb library, and they help us answer letters. Rather than write a personal letter, to someone with a gardenia problem, we slip a bulletin, *How To Grow Gardenias*, into the self-addressed, stamped envelope they send us. The leaflet gives more information than we would if we wrote a personal letter. Sometimes our leaflets do not cover a certain question, then we answer the letter personally. Here again the answer is short and sweet and full of meat, for example: "Dear friend. Your Impatiens plant has aphids or plant lice. Spray with malathion, 1 teaspoon to 2 qts. of water, once every 2 weeks, with a pinch of soap added. Best wishes, Green Thumb."

11. *Don't Leave Any Stone Unturned!* Study trade magazines such as *Editor and Publisher* and *Writer's Digest.* Get the feel for markets and get editor's names.

When a salesman from radio station WHAM (50,000 Watt), Rochester, N.Y. asked us if we would be interested in doing a Green Thumb radio show, Katy and I grabbed at the chance, following the same format of "short and sweet and full of meat."

We're happy to share our experiences with fellow readers of the *Writer's Digest.* Naturally, we don't guarantee you can go right out and start your own syndicated feature merely by following our footsteps and suggestions. An old farmer once told us, "It's the man, and not the land" that makes the successful farmer. The same applies to writing or any other endeavor. Writing takes a lot of effort and hard work, but with 130 dailies and weeklies under our belt, we proved it *can be* done.

# How to Write and Sell Light Verse

## Don't just send those short poems of yours to friends —Sell them to editors!

*by Jean Conder Soule*

WITH NEARLY 2000 light verses published, I think it safe to say that anyone who has a sense of humor, a feeling for rhyme and rhythm, and the ability to cope with puns and punch lines can eventually write salable light verse. Using the trial and error method (with more errors than I'd care to mention) I have finally seen my poems in such well-known spots as the "Pepper and Salt" column of the *Wall Street Journal,* the "Parting Shots" section of the *American Legion Magazine,* and until its departure from the scene, in the *Saturday Evening Post's* renowned, "Post Scripts."

Now I'd be the first one to admit that my first efforts in this field met with little or no success. It has taken hours of patient rewriting, reworking titles and punch lines, condensing those 16 lines to 8, and much manual labor to market my wares. Today, however, I can look back over almost 12 years of sales and tell you that my scrapbook is bulging with clippings and my savings account is finally beginning to prosper. If you have a natural flair for the humorous; a feeling for clever rhyming and an instinct about the subject matter which makes the best theme for light verses, you can sell, too. There are a few ground rules you need to know in the writing and selling of this particular type of poetry (yes, I dare to call it that!) and I'll be glad to share them with you.

*First:* Remember that your poem must have an instantaneous response and a universal appeal. Your reader must "get the point" immediately or the light verse dies a-borning. In this kind of writing, reader identification and feeling of "rapport" between writer and reader is of the utmost importance. So, if you are to produce this reaction, you must write about life as you know it, life as you live it with all its frustrations, daily pitfalls and human failings.

I would urge you to listen carefully to what other people say on trains, trolleys, subways, in the supermarket—wherever you happen to be. Study the person next to you on the bus or the woman seated near you at the PTA meeting. Tuck away in your memory little catch phrases and humorous remarks you hear at parties or kaffee klatches. You never know when one of these fragments may become the subject for your next poem.

*Second:* Keep your poem *short.* Brevity is indeed the soul of wit and this is doubly true in light verse. If you can give your reader a complete, well-rounded thought in 8 lines instead of 16, or if you can compress an idea from 8 lines into a charming humorous quatrain, chances are you'll have a much better poem. Chances also are that you'll sell it. Unfortunately much of the light verse published today in magazines and newspapers is used as filler material. There are some magazines which devote whole pages to light verse (such as *Mature Years,* 201 8th Avenue S., Nashville, Tenn.), but most editors just won't give that much space to poetry.

*Third:* Use well-known verse forms for your light verse. Don't try to be inventive in this department. Couplets and quatrains are your best bets. Occasionally a magazine will use a limerick or a triolet, but I'd advise you to stick to the more common everyday garden variety of verse forms—at least until your name is well-known in the field.

Quatrains are always popular and if yours is good enough, an editor will have a hard time turning it down. If you can rhyme the first and third lines as well as the second and fourth, the editor will consider you a real "pro", but many quatrains simply rhyme the second and fourth. For example, in this one originally published in the Canadian women's magazine, *Chatelaine,* I said:

### ROOM SERVICE

I'd love to be leisurely every day
　　If I had the chance to employ it.
But the only time I get breakfast in bed
　　Is when I'm too sick too enjoy it.

An example of the light verse couplet is:

NOT TO MY CREDIT
I could say "Charge-it" in a flash;
But I'm long on credit—and short on cash

*Fourth:* The *title* should give an additional humorous touch to your light verse. Remember, the title is the first thing an editor will see, so make it just as perfect as you can. Be sure to make the title fit the poem without giving away your punch line. If the editor reads your verse and says, "By golly, that's good, and the title is just right," then I'll bet you two to one you've made a sale.

Puns are quite popular in titles and I must admit I use them a great deal. The shorter the title, the better. Brevity counts here, too, and unless you're deliberately trying to come up with a long, humorous title to set off your poem, better leave lengthy involved titles for people who write prose.

To give you some examples of titles which helped to sell my light verse, here are just a few. In a poem about raking leaves in the fall (and most of the leaves were his neighbor's), I titled it "Fall Guy." In a light verse which made the "Pepper and Salt" column of the *Wall Street Journal* just recently, I described my displeasure at being at the beach with three small children who collected too much sand. The title was "Against the Grain." Referring to the way in which our teenager labors in winter for snowbound neighbors but leaves *us* isolated till the paying jobs are over. I called my poem "Snow Job."

The *fifth* rule I would give you is this: give your peom the very best punch line you can think of. Your last line should be the lightest and brightest in your entire poem. Often it comes as a surprise and is a complete reversal of what you have been saying. However you do it, be sure your punch line adds a special little "twist" at the end which brings an additional chuckle. Perhaps this quatrain on dieting will show you what I mean:

LOSING BATTLE
Dieting's rough.
By my own admission
The first thing I lose
Is my disposition!

Again quoting from my favorite newspaper, here's one with a real surprise ending:

VACATION FORECAST
The bathing's delightful;
The fishing is great.
The sailing is perfect,
The hiking first-rate.

The weather is golden,
Days sunny and fair—
Excepting, of course,
The week that we're there!

Now, as a final hint to all of you light verse writers (may your tribe increase!), let me add this bit of advice. If you can find a new and amusing way to phrase your words—even though your subject-matter may be as old as the hills—then you may very well come up with a snappy, witty, and clever poem which no editor can bear to part with. The phrase, "There's nothing new under the sun" is all too true, but there certainly are *new ways* of saying the same old thing. It's up to us light verse writers to find those new ways, and if we do, we can't lose!

# 10 Tips for Writing and Selling Children's Plays

*Does today's TV child still respond to the magic of live theater? Yes, but when writing for him, remember these rules*

*by David Dean Wenstrom as told to M. C. McCrory*

W HEN I WRITE a children's play I think about the audience. It is probably wearing snowpants, has lost its Aunt Velma's telephone number and is greeting loud friends seven rows back. If it is awed by the slow dimming of the auditorium lights and curious about the pachyderm drape of the stage curtains, so far so good. The children's play had better start with a bang or a whisper, a blaze or a blackness, a happening there and then.

Whether they are four years old or in fourth grade, the children did not come to be taught, trained, scathed or bewitched: they came to be entertained. I have watched the children's theatre audience since 1937 and I believe writers and producers sometimes had a wrong idea of what entertains children. They thought the theatre was for precocious and precious types, an exotic reward for exquisite behavior.

Instead, theatre is a creative experience long before print hits foolscap and long after the last clap sends the knowing actor home . . . a creation that children especially can share. It is play-acting, the fun, frolic and might-have-been. Stop right now and think of the children you have watched watching *The Mouse That Roared, The Wizard of Oz, Aladdin and His Lamp.*

Children are eager to believe what the actor and director want them to—just suggest what is happening. One minute a prince is standing beside an open window. There is a clap of thunder, an instant of darkness. The lights then show, through the open window, a flying swan. After that, the actors only point to where the swans are in the sky or a shadow crosses the sunset sky. A fairy godmother does not "walk on" but appears by the director's magic. The writer should write in the situation for a flash and a cloud of smoke, or a blaze of rainbow lights—never a plodding fairy godmother. *That* the children have enough sense to laugh at. So make *it* a comedy.

The slow evolution of worthwhile children's plays is not always the writer's fault. The mechanics of theatre are complicated. A play should first be fully prepared for use, a true playscript, complete. Those suitable last an hour or longer. The writer makes every effort to have his play produced: in his hometown, at the "Y," in college experimental groups, children's theatre organizations, in contests or at church. The actors should be the best available, the children need be nothing of the kind. If the play catches the children's attention at several intervals, if the actors are eager, if the producer is especially full of suggestions, the writer had better try to market the play.

Marketing is done by sending it consecutively to the few tough-necked, light-hearted people who publish plays for children's theatre. A play does not make money for anybody unless it is produced. Manuscripts are usually bought on a royalty-contract basis. The publisher risks the cost of putting the play into print and advertising it, generally in a catalog. The producer sends for a play-book; is pleased with what he reads and imagines, sends for enough play-books for each member of his cast. Once the play is ready to be seen, every time it is given before an audience, whether that audience pays or not, the stated royalty must be sent to the publisher. This may be $5.00 or it may be $50 for every performance. (Non-royalty plays exist where the publisher has bought a script outright and sells the play-book only.)

The writer will eventually reap his contracted share from a play he carefully wrote, steered into a successful performance, and eventually sold to a publisher who thought it was worth offering to the rather wistful producers of children's theatre.

I'm a producer, yet I've found myself writing—I could say *having* to write—sixteen plays for children. Thirteen of my plays are dramatizations based on well-known fairy tales and three are originals. We are speaking, of course, of plays written to entertain children and presented by adult actors. For thirty years I have been either staging, directing, performing or writing plays and in that time I have observed the audience reaction.

I can think of ten things I learned for myself both as a playwright and a producer, that might help the new writer.

## Tips for Playwrights

1. A child laughs at behavior, not ideas.
2. State an idea at least three times or three ways, in hopes that the audience will catch it.
3. I measure the success of a play by the attention the children pay to it. One must write attention-getters into any third line of a play. Or let's say the odd and even lines.
4. Liven the language of the play. A child will listen to new words even if they are in a foreign language. Give him this enrichment. The actions or the characterizations point up the meaning of the words.
5. Delight must mitigate horror. In other words, it is fun to be scared and plays for children can be full of delightful horrors.
6. The child gets his security from a sense of magic. Let him see the wand early in the play, that magic which is available to make everything come out all right. (By the way, honesty is a lot more essential to the security of children than is "happiness-ever-after.")
7. Do not go beyond the conceptions of a child but do not underestimate the audience. More and more, every year, theatre will be offered to children who are not precocious in intelligence but who are used to the extravagances of TV. Find new ways to tell a child the things he already knows or senses.
8. Children love beauty. Point up the spots of beauty your play can give to children and then trust the director to provide the technical details. I like to work bare-stage myself, but I revel in lightings. When mass would be more realistic I have turned to the diminutive and wheeled small jewelled castles and little cardboard Jersey cows onto the stage. A princess should have shimmering clothes, nothing makeshift or impoverished. Write lavish beauty into the plays.

9. The didactic, the moralistic, the satiric, the cynical, even the sentimental is lost on children. If he is listening at all to your play a child is hearing *dialogue made visible*.

10. Allow the child-audience into the play. There are never four walls to the stage. If the actor senses that the audience is well ahead of the play he can say so:—"We know what's going to happen, don't we," he states as he looks across the pit to the impatient audience, "but I'll bet you don't know where Reekwrather Skullbone found the stones to put into that sack. I see one. Let's watch the old chicken thief find it. Quiet now."

The playwright must see and hear every moment of his play through a child's senses. He must anticipate action by placing dialogue where it will cast its shadow in an act. On the stage action and the dialogue move together.

### We Need You, Writers!

Somebody should be writing new plays for children. It might as well be you. There are more organizations eager to put on plays to entertain children and to give adult actors worthwhile parts than there are plays to select from. When a play is produced, every time it is produced, it earns a fixed royalty for the publisher and the writer. Producers have to pay these royalties whether the play is written well for the child audience or leaves it fidgety and unaware of anything new in experience.

Before starting to write *your* play *for* children, look again at the real audience. Besides the stolid snowpants it is probably wearing a one-cent ring and calling it "magic." The child is already writing a play to suit himself.

### Children's plays have names like:

*Ali Baba and the Forty Thieves*

*Alice in Wonderland*

*Arthur and the Magic Sword*

*Buffalo Bill* (historical saga, told in dramatic action and dance mime.)

*Crazy Cricket Farm* (a modern comedy, vividly portraying middle-western farm life in America. 4 women, 2 men, 6 children. Two sets. Modern costumes.)

*Flibberty Gibbet, His Last Chance* (a delicate fantasy, adapted from a Scottish folk tale.)

*Hiawatha, Peacemaker of the Iroquois* (developed from history by James Norris. 3 women, 13 men. (Three sets. Indian costumes.)

*The Land of the Dragon* (stylized Chinese play, done in the ancient and delightful Chinese manner. 5 women, 3 men, 1 dragon.)

# Freelance Job Opportunity: Review Writing

## Combine Your Writing and Critical Skills for Publisher's Check

### by James Boeringer

As a craftsman of the art of writing, you may also be interested and informed in the fields of drama, music or the visual arts, as well. Why not combine your writing skill with another artistic field you also know, and market your criticisms? New books, plays, musicals, concerts, lectures, exhibits, all provide material for you.

Your own qualifications, besides your ability to write, are, first, enough knowledge of your subject to earn the respect of your peers, and, second, enough genuine enthusiasm to assure a lively and personable reaction to what you see and hear.

### Have a Main Idea

A measure of standard journalism enters into critical writing. Most editors will insist that paragraphs be short and that the standard who-what-when-where questions be covered in the first paragraph. You should also make the main idea of your review immediately clear. This main idea should summarize the succession of aesthetic experiences the event offered.

For example, in reviewing an exhibit of op art or trompe l'oeuil paintings, the unalert critic might simply describe the optical illusions of the works and state whether or not he liked the tricks they played with his eyes, while the more perceptive writer would realize and point out that the highly demanding brush techniques of such works runs against the loose and undisciplined techniques of the past twenty years.

This central idea allows the writer to move logically and pointedly through his descriptions and evaluations, pulling them together. If his lead paragraph has stated the idea in an arresting way, his chain of supporting observations can hold the reader all the way to the end.

## Be Brief

If you wind up criticizing staged events for a daily paper, there is another practical advantage to the "main idea" approach, lying in the fact that your night editor will hold a limited amount of space open for you until a specific deadline time.

This usually gives you about 12 column inches or 350 words, and anywhere from 30 minutes to an hour in which to compose them.

It would probably be easier to write a thousand words in that time, because anybody can write a lot of bad material fast. The "main idea" helps you to keep your material short and to the point, and filling unused space is easy. If the editor does have to cut without consulting you, he will prune later subsidiary material instead of your main criticisms.

Still another advantage is the fact that you will get better headlines. You do not get to write your own heads; this is done by the night-editor or by a head-writer who has been trained to distill his words from your opening paragraph. So get right to the point.

If you ramble at the beginning, you may wind up with a head like "New Play Fails" for a review that later on expresses the opposite idea. Your readers always think you wrote the head, even though you have no control over it; so "main idea" criticism is a good way to avoid embarrassment.

A detail of format: your review is always the last thing to come in, and if you have left no space for the head, then the editor, who is probably harried by that time, has to paste half a sheet at the top of your page. So start halfway down, and triple-space.

There is seldom a by-line for criticism; instead, you type your name at the end. Some papers use only initials.

## Maintain Your Own Viewpoint

Just as in fiction a clear "viewpoint" must be maintained, so in a review it is your own ideas that you must put across, not the general reaction of the audience, or what you overhear intelligent-sounding people saying in the lobby.

By all means report an audience reaction if it is a striking one like a standing ovation or twenty curtain calls, but if you are convinced that such a reaction was only misdirected mob impulsiveness, say so, and give your reasons. By the same token, never be afraid to be enthusiastic about an event that seemed to leave everybody else cold, if you really felt that way.

## Be Clear

Never assume your reader has been there. It is up to you to recreate the event and to put your own interpretation across with crystal clarity.

The reason for this is that criticism must be readable and meaningful in the complete absence of the event being discussed. The arts supply the springboard, but the criticism must acquire an independent existence and an importance all its own. What it has to say must be permanently valid and interesting.

This is why the writings of really great critics like Max Beerbohm and George Bernard Shaw are republished to be read and reread long after the things they discussed have faded away.

## How to Sell

Let's suppose you have done some practicing at reviewing, and you have sharpened your skill in grasping and expressing a main idea briefly, clearly, and from your own interesting viewpoint. Now how do you sell your material?

You might start with a weekly paper. Reviewable events tend to occur on weekends, and weeklies tend to come out on Thursdays. That fact eliminates the rush of the dailies.

Go to the editor and talk over the project with him. Chances are he has to do almost everything by himself. He has probably been pestered by the local Artists' Series committee to give them more coverage, and will be glad to pay anywhere from $1 to $5 for your work, to which you can add the value of the brace of free tickets you'll get, which are always for excellent seats.

Working as a correspondent for a national trade magazine in the arts is much like working for a weekly newspaper, in that there is no pressure. In this case, you write a sample summary review of a month's important arts events in your area and submit it with a query. It's difficult for a New York or Chicago trade magazine to maintain a corps of writers all over the country, and there is sometimes an opening. Such magazines pay as little as they can, say $5 a release to start, but as you prove your own value, you can earn up to $50 or more per summary.

After apprenticeship on weeklies or as a trade magazine correspondent, you can move on to a daily. Read the local papers carefully, and ascertain which are not covering arts events at all or are sending unwilling news reporters to cover them. Then submit your query and sample to the editor or publisher.

You can also work through the ordinary personnel office. I secured an excellent series of assignments on the *Daily Oklahoman* simply by going to the personnel office and filling out the usual forms, putting down "music critic" in the blank "type of position desired." The mere fact that there was no established file of such applications may have brought mine to the attention of the editor.

Dailies pay better than weeklies or magazines. The lowest figure you should take would be $5 per review, and you can get up to about $30, depending upon the circulation of the paper and the experience and appeal you can offer. Beyond that figure, the work turns into a salaried position.

Reviews of books and records are sometimes harder to sell to newspapers unless there is some sort of pressure from a big advertiser or the paper runs a regular arts feature section that needs a personal hometown touch.

Magazines are a better field for that kind of reviewing, and you can be sure that there are periodicals devoted to every field in which you may have special knowledge, from chess to children. Look over your specialized magazines, see which ones lack review-columns, and submit a query and a sample of your work. You may land a fascinating job as a columnist that will pay $5 to $50 a shot, while you build up your library for free.

Write directly to publishers for review copies of specific books, stating briefly the nature and circulation of your magazine. Send tear-sheets of your published reviews to the co-operating publishers.

## Freelancing

Freelancing criticism is easy if you are alert to good subjects, which are, chiefly, world premieres, arts festivals, significant revivals, and local-color events. The pattern of these critical articles is somewhat different from simple criticism, since you must intersperse lively, revealing anecdotes through your discussion and comments.

A world premiere is, of course, the first time some artistic thing is revealed to the public. It may be commissioned music, a new mural or monument, or the first performance of a drama that has some connection with your area.

A festival is a complicated, co-operative venture devoted to a specific segment of the arts. For freelancing purposes, the more unusual and fresh the segment, the better—and the more marketable.

I happened to be in South Dakota during the revival of the first opera ever written west of the Mississippi (it was by General Custer's bandmaster); the uniqueness of the work and the odd combination of opera with frontier life sold it to the Sunday *New York Times*.

Local color sold another of my critical articles to the *Times*. This time it was about an avant-garde theatre in Oklahoma, a state more likely to be associated with the oil wells that stand on its capitol grounds.

Photographs should accompany all these freelance features, since they increase the value of your pieces, which should range from $75 to $250 upwards, depending upon the scope and significance of your material.

## Tips and Warnings

Stick to professionals. In reviewing amateur work, you have the unpleasant choice of compromising your standards or infuriating a segment of your public, which is bound to have a rosy view of local "talent."

Keep in mind that interviews with visiting artists are salable. Every new article about a celebrity helps his career. He knows this, and will be willing to take time to talk to you. Take some photos, or get them from the artist's agent.

Be prepared to be criticized yourself. Your well-wishers will keep quiet; so most of your mail will be fairly virulent. Reply only if you feel the criticisms are valid.

Don't become intoxicated with your own power. Coming in print repeatedly with your opinions can give you a rather heady view of your own sagacity, which can spoil your writing with smugness, sarcasm, or condescension. Your job is to seek out and express aesthetic truth, not to inflate your own ego.

Be positive of your facts. You're safe if you say, "Madame Tessitura sounded as if she had a cold." But if you say, "Madame Tessitura certainly had a bad cold," she can sue you, and only a doctor's certification of the cold will get you out of it.

Keep up your sense of humor. Go along with the funny things that keep happening in the arts. Recognize the importance of what you are doing, but don't take yourself or your job too seriously. Besides being profitable, criticism should provide the healthy, enjoyable satisfaction that any other kind of real creative writing provides.

# The Mechanics of Writing

*by Allan Eckert*

IT'S A GRAND THING to dream of seeing a story with your by-line in one of the major national magazines. The actual *writing* of it may be a bit difficult, but once you have it down in good shape on a rough draft, the rest is a snap . . . you *think*. There is still one very important—though often irksome—chore to do.

Sometimes it's a little difficult to climb off that lofty, creative plane of writing and find the old bugaboo of simple manuscript mechanics staring you in the eye. It's a comedown. It's irritating. It's bothersome. But it's a necessary evil and the quicker you start using the right way, the easier it is to live with.

## Type of Paper

One of the things to consider is the paper you'll use for that final draft. There are only two hard and fast rules: it must be white paper and it must measure 8½ x 11 inches. That's a standard size and editors are adamant; they don't want off-beat colors and sizes.

There's a wide range of white, 8½ x 11 papers. The cheaper ones are all wood content. They'll suffice but they're not recommended. They tear easily, are highly absorbent and have a fuzzy texture which causes type to blur. They cost about $2.75 per ream (500 sheets.)

At the opposite end are fine, slick, 100 per cent rag content papers which are beautiful . . . and expensive. Unless you have money to burn, they're impractical, as they'll run to $12 or more per ream.

The best bet seems to be a good 25 per cent cotton fiber content paper. It has quality feel, smoothness, shows type neatly and holds up under erasing. This type can also be purchased with the extra benefit of special treatment which makes it easy to erase typing errors with just a flick of a pencil eraser. The cost is about $6.75 per ream for the easy erase paper and about $5.90 per ream for the regular untreated paper.

Where weight of the paper is concerned, don't use under a 16-pound bond, and 20-pound is preferred.

### Carbon Copies

You don't *have* to make any carbon copies, but you're wise to do it. If your story gets lost somewhere, it doesn't become a disaster. Sometimes, too, you'll find you have particular needs for extra carbon copies—for editors of reprint magazines, for friends, for marking your own copy for revision, etc. It is highly recommended that at least one carbon copy be made, possibly two or three if you think they'll be needed. A medium-weight carbon paper ($4.00 per box of 100 sheets) is good. Your carbon copy sheets (often called second sheets) can be cheaper grade mimeo paper of a different color. To save room and expense and get better copies, duplicate copy paper (very thin) can be used. Your choice.

### Type Characters

Another firm rule: for manuscript typing, use only elite or pica type. The slightly larger pica type is easier to read and editors like it, but they don't object to elite. They *do* dislike (and often will refuse) hard-to-read or unusual typewritten characters, such as script, italics, Old English, all capitals, unusual letter styles, etc. If you're sending out manuscripts typed with one of these, there's a solid strike against you before a word is read.

### Layout of Page One

You should not use a cover sheet and, while you don't absolutely *have* to follow this style of manuscript preparation, it's a standard editors prefer, so give 'em what they're looking for.

In the upper left hand corner should be your name, street address and city-zone-state on three single-spaced lines. Nothing in upper center. It is *not* necessary to indicate that this is Page One. At upper right, approximate wordage and, especially with fiction, the rights you're offering for sale—single-spaced in three lines.

## How to Estimate Wordage

To estimate wordage, count the exact number of words on the first three pages of your manuscript (in manuscripts up to 25 pages), divide the total by 3 and multiple the result by the number of pages. Carry the total to the nearest 100 words. For example, say you have a 12-page manuscript with totals of 182, 316 and 289 words on the first three pages. Divide your total of 787 by 3 to get 262. Now multiply 262 x 12 pages and you get 3,144. Your approximate wordage, therefore, will be 3,100 words. On manuscripts over 25 pages, count five pages instead of three, then follow the same process, dividing by 5 instead of 3.

Now, flip the lever to double-space and center the title (preferably in upper and lower case, rather than all capitals) halfway down the page. To center, set the tabulator to stop in the exact left-right center of the page. Count the letters in the title (including spaces and punctuation) and backspace half that number. Centered one double-space under that, type "by" and centered one double-space under that, your name or pseudonym.

Margins should be 1 to 2 inches on the left and 1 to 1¼ on the right. Bottom margin should be at least one inch. Paragraph indentation should be five letterspaces.

Now, after the title and byline block, drop down three double-spaces, paragraph indent and start your story.

## Pages After Page One

On the upper left of every page after page one, type your last name. In the upper center, the page number (for example, page sixteen would be typed − 16 −). At the upper right, type the title or, if it's too long, then a keyword to the title. A keyword for this article, for instance, might simply be . . . Mechanics . . .

To begin copy on each page after page one, drop down four or five double-spaces. Margins remain the same as on page one.

## Concluding Page of the Manuscript

Carry on just as you have on other pages after page one. After your last word and period on this page, however, skip two or three double spaces and then center the words "The End" or, more commonly, the old telegrapher's symbol of—30—, meaning the same thing.

### Special Points to Keep in Mind

Always use a good dark black (*not* colored) typewriter ribbon and clean your keys frequently. If the enclosures in the letters a, b, d, e, g, etc. get inked-in, your keys need cleaning. Keep your manuscript neat *always*. Occasional retyping over erasures is acceptable, but strike-overs are bad and give a manuscript a very sloppy, careless appearance. Most editors won't object too much if manuscripts under eight pages are folded in thirds and letter-mailed. However, there is a marked *preference* for flat mailing (in large envelopes) of manuscripts over four pages. *Never* staple your manuscript pages together. Use a paperclip only.

### Illustrations

Where you will be enclosing illustrations (photographs or art work) with your piece, make sure that each example has your name and address rubber-stamped or lightly pencilled (never typed or written with ballpoint pen) in one corner on the back. A stiff piece of cardboard larger than the largest illustration should be used to prevent damage. The manuscript and photos can be held to it with rubber bands. The outer envelope should be stamped or block-lettered: PHOTOS—DO NOT BEND OR FOLD. Even if you don't send illustrations, it's a good idea to attach your manuscript to the backing either with rubber bands or paperclip to prevent bending and to keep the manuscript fresh and neat.

### Mailing Envelopes

For best results and least cost in the long run, buy the large gummed or clasped mailing envelopes in the 100-size box at about $5.50. You'll need two sizes—9 x 12 for the return envelope and 9½ x 12½ or 10 x 13 for the one used to send out the manuscript, photos and return envelope. Small (4 x 2½) address labels to stick on the envelopes after they are typed out makes a neat appearance.

## Mailing Your Manuscript

Except when working under direct assignment from a magazine, *always* enclose with your manuscript a self-addressed return envelope with the correct amount of postage stamps on it.

Mark your envelope, as desired, with FIRST CLASS MAIL, or SPECIAL FOURTH CLASS RATE: MANUSCRIPT. First Class Mail costs 6¢ per ounce but assures better handling and faster delivery. Special Fourth Class Rate costs 12¢ for the first pound and 6¢ for each additional pound or fraction. Special Fourth Class mail is handled the same as Parcel Post so wrap it well. Also, the Special Fourth Class rate only applies in the U.S.A.

For lighter weight manuscripts, First Class mail is recommended because of the better speed and handling. Most First Class mail going any distance is flown on a space available basis.

Insurance is available, but payable only on the tangible value of what is in the package, i.e., writing paper, so your best insurance is to keep a copy at home of what you send.

First Class mail is forwarded or returned automatically, however. Special Fourth Class Rate mail is not. To make sure you get your submission back if undeliverable, print "Return Postage Guaranteed" under your return address.

You may enclose a personal letter with your manuscript sent at the Special Fourth Class Rate, but you must also add enough First Class postage to cover the letter (usually 6¢) and mark FIRST CLASS LETTER ENCLOSED on the outside.

In most cases, you should *not* include a personal letter unless you have something very pertinent to say. Nothing you can say in a letter will sell the manuscript if the piece won't stand up by itself without a letter. The exception may be where the piece has been written after first receiving a go-ahead from the editor in response to a prior query. Then you may wish to nudge his memory that this is the piece he wanted to see. Keep it brief, something like this:

Dear Mr. _____
Enclosed you'll find the article we previously discussed, entitled "(title)." I trust you'll find it suitable for your use.

Sincerely yours,

But you really *shouldn't* enclose a letter with a manuscript going out cold (i.e., without prior query.) However, if you *do*,
keep it short and to the point; something like:

> Dear Mr. _____
> I've slanted my enclosed story, "(title)," specifically toward
> your publication and you may find it just right for your
> needs.
>
> Sincerely yours,

## Mailing Book Manuscripts

Do not bind your book pages in any way. They should be
mailed loose in a box (a stationery box is ideal) without covers,
stapling, binding, clasping or ties of any kind. Unless you enclose sufficient return postage, many publishing houses, if they
reject it, will return it to you by Express Collect—and that's
expensive!

Be sure to reinforce the corners of your mailing box with
tape to help prevent bursting or crushing in handling. It is
*always* a good idea to insure the book manuscript. If it gets lost,
at least the cost of the big retyping job is paid for.

Seal the lid of the box to the bottom with several small pieces
of transparent tape and then neatly wrap and seal the box in
brown mailing paper. Type out and attach your mailing labels.
You can, if you wish, mail the package by Parcel Post or Air
Express instead of EM if you like, but they are more expensive
rates.

If you enclose a letter in the box, state this on the outer wrapping and add an additional 6¢ stamp to the EM postal rate. You
can, if you like, put the letter into a stamped envelope and se-
curely tape this to the outside of the package.

## Easy as Driving

While all of these different phases of the mechanics of manuscript preparation may at first leave you a little confused, before long they'll come to you as naturally as driving, where
you won't even have to give them a thought to do the job right.

There are few hard and fast rules, but the tips and recom-
mendations made here show what the editors prefer. Do it cor-
rectly right from the start, give the editors what they prefer

and you won't be beginning with a strike or two against you before the manuscript is even read.

## PREPARING YOUR MANUSCRIPT

Your name goes here
Your address here

State here the rights that
you are offering for sale.
Number of words goes here.
Page number here

### TITLE OF STORY GOES HERE
By
Your Name or Pseudonym

The story or article begins about halfway down the first page. It should be typed double-spaced. In the upper right hand corner should appear the approximate number of words. Every word counts. The word "a" counts as a word. Abbreviated words count as one word. Count the exact number of words on three pages, and from that compute the number in the manuscript. In a longer script, of say 50 pages, you should count exactly the number of words on 5 pages and compute the total from that.

Each subsequent page should be numbered and carry your last name, preferably on the top left hand corner of the page. (The number goes at top right hand corner.) Use either pica or elite type. There is no editorial preference. Be sure though, to use a clean ribbon, and keep typewriter keys cleaned. Your script must be neat. Scripts under 5 pages should be folded in thirds; longer scripts should be mailed flat. Always use 8½ x 11" white paper. Stay away from any paper, typewriting, or ribbon that is "offcolor."

Be sure to type only on one side of the sheet. Any drawings, tables or photographs should be keyed by letter or number to the appropriate manuscript area.

Leave a margin of about 1 inch on all sides.

Always enclose sufficient return postage on a self-addressed envelope.

### How Do You Submit . . . ?

*Short articles,* poems, stories of less than five pages in length may be folded in threes and submitted in a no. 10 envelope to most magazines; everything should be typed double spaced on 8½ x 11 white paper. Type poems one to a page. Always enclose a self-addressed envelope and return postage.

*Longer articles,* stories of more than five pages in length should be submitted flat in a 9 x 12 or 10 x 13 envelope with another self-addressed envelope enclosed and return postage.

*Book length* manuscripts should be submitted loose in a manuscript paper box. Although a few book publishers prefer to receive manuscripts held together in a binder of some sort, the majority of editors feel it is too heavy to hold to read comfortably. Always enclose sufficient postage for the manuscript's return.

*Photographs* and other illustrative materials should always be submitted flat, of course, with cardboard protectors and sufficient return postage. In the case of small filler items, a few trade journals and hobby books will accept (although they do not prefer) Polaroid shots of the item in question.

*Play manuscripts* should be submitted bound in a flexible binder of some sort, along with sufficient return postage. A few publishers of one-act plays have indicated that for the very *short* lengths they have no objection to the materials submitted flat, held only by a paperclip.

*Television* and motion picture scripts should be submitted in a soft cover binder with sufficient return postage.

*Greeting card ideas* and gag ideas for cartoonists should be submitted on 3 x 5 white slips of paper, flat, with sufficient return postage. The writer's name and address should appear in the upper left-hand corner and the gag idea or verse centered on the page. A code number for convenience in identifying the gag idea or verse in correspondence should appear in the upper right-hand corner. Studio and humorous card ideas may also be accompanied by a rough drawing on a separate folded sheet of paper similar to the published card. Always enclose stamped, self-addressed envelope.

## THE WAITING GAME

The free-lance writer who sends off a story or an article to a magazine usually turns to the other ideas on his desk and temporarily forgets about his submission. But one day he realizes it's been too long since he heard anything from his brainchild.

He wonders if, whether he inquires about it, he'll be jeopardizing a possible sale. Are they really considering it or has the editor had an accident and it's at the bottom of a big stack of unread mail? Maybe it was lost?

As a thumbnail guide to the writer who wants to know when it's safe to requery an editor about his manuscript, WRITER'S DIGEST lists below the average reporting times of publishers and agents and some suggestions for follow-up letters:

|  | *Average reporting time* |
| --- | --- |
| Magazine | Six weeks to two months |
| Book Publisher | Two to three months |
| Literary Agent | Three weeks to two months |
| Literary Critic | Short material: three weeks<br>Book length: two months |

If you've had no report from a publisher by the maximum reporting time given above, just write a brief inquiry letter to the editor asking if your manuscript or article query (and give the story title or a brief description of the article) is still under consideration. It's a good idea to enclose a self-addressed stamped envelope with this letter too, to expedite a reply. (And, of course, your original submission must *always* include sufficient return postage.)

In the rare case, where a publisher fails to report even after your inquiry, write a registered letter to the editor, advising that you are withdrawing your manuscript from that publication's consideration for resubmission elsewhere. Then retype an original copy of the manuscript and resubmit it to another market. Also, send the details to WRITER'S DIGEST, so we can follow up with the publisher in question and check against possible other complaints in our files. If the facts warrant, we will then publish appropriate notices in WRITER'S DIGEST.

Contacting your agent is a different matter. He is more than likely to be in touch with you as soon as he has anything to report and prefers to be spending his time contacting possible buyers for you than answering letters or phone calls from his clients. But when you feel a report is overdue, don't hesitate to write him a brief note.

# Miscellany Market Sampler

**Here are more than 100 places to sell what you write.**

# Consumer Publications

**THE AMERICAN LEGION MAGAZINE,** 1345 Ave. of Americas, New York, N.Y. 10019. Monthly. ABC audited circulation 2.6 million. $2 yearly via Circulation Dept. P.O. Box 1954, Indianapolis, Ind. 46206. Reports on most submissions promptly, borderline decisions take time. Buys first North American serial rights. Pays on acceptance. Include phone number with ms. Enclose S.A.S.E.* for ms return.

**Nonfiction:** Most articles written on order. Some over transom. Writers may query for subject interest, but no assignments to writers unknown to editors. Subjects include national and international affairs, American history, reader self-interest, great military campaigns and battles, major aspects of American life, etc. Average length 15-20 double spaced typewritten pages. Pay varies widely with length and worth of work. Research assignments for some skilled reporters. Proven pro's only.
**Photos:** Chiefly on assignment. Very rarely an over-transom pic story or photo clicks.

**Poetry and Humor:** Limited market for short light verse, and short humorous anecdotes, epigrams, jokes, etc. No serious verse, Taboos: old material; bad taste; amateurish work. Short humorous verse: $2.50 per line, minimum $10. Epigrams: $10. Anecdotes $20. Submissions must be typewritten.

**ARIZONA WILDLIFE SPORTSMAN,** 1103 North Central, Phoenix, Ariz. 85004. Editor: Bob Hirsch. 50¢ monthly. Circulation: 17,000. Reports in one month. Not copyrighted. Buys first North American serial rights. Pays on publication. Enclose S.A.S.E. for ms return.

**Nonfiction:** Material on hunting, fishing, camping, boating,

* S.A.S.E. refers to Self-Addressed, Stamped Envelope.

wildlife, conservation and other outdoor subjects, provided they are applicable to Southwest conditions. Especially interested in how-to-do-it, where-to-do-it and experience pieces complete with photos or drawings. Personal experiences of an informative nature are also accepted. Rates vary. Query first.

**Photos:** Buy pix with mss. Deals with the outdoors—wild animals and birds of the Southwest. High quality b&w, 5x7 or 8x10 glossy. Pays $3 and up. Subjects should be in sharp definition.

**THE ATLANTIC,** 8 Arlington St., Boston, Mass. 02116. Editor: Robert Manning. 75¢ monthly. Copyrighted. Circulation 350,000. To a professional, academic audience. Buys first North American serial rights. Reporting time, two weeks to several months. Pays on acceptance. Will send sample copy for 75¢. Enclose S.A.S.E. for ms return.

**Nonfiction:** "We prefer not to formulate specifications about the desired content of the Atlantic and suggest that would-be contributors examine back issues to form their own judgment of what is suitable." Lengths, 2,000 to 5,000 words. Rates vary from $100 per magazine page base rate. Author should include summary of his qualifications for treating subject.

**Fiction:** Short stories by unestablished writers, published as Atlantic "Firsts" are a steady feature. Two prizes of $750 and $250 are awarded annually to the best of these. Candidates should so label their submissions and list their previous publications, if any, as authors whose stories have appeared in magazines of national circulation are not considered eligible. Will also consider stories by established writers in lengths ranging from 2,700 to 7,500 words. Payment depends on length, but also on quality and author.

**Poetry:** Uses three to five poems an issue. These must be of high literary distinction in both light and serious poetry. Interested in the work of young poets. Base rate for poetry is $2 per line.

**BARRON'S NATIONAL BUSINESS AND FINANCIAL WEEK-LY,** 30 Broad St., New York, N.Y. 10004. Editor: Robert Bleiberg. This is a 50¢ weekly for business and investment people. Will send free sample copy to a writer on request. Buys all rights. Pays on publication. Enclose S.A.S.E. for ms return.

**Nonfiction:** Articles 2,000 words or more, about various industries with investment point of view; shorter articles on particular companies, their past performance and future prospects as related to industry trends for "News and Views" column. Pays $150 to $300 for articles; $60-$75 for "News and Views" material. Articles considered on speculation only.

**CAR LIFE,** 1499 Monrovia Ave., Newport Beach, Calif. 92663. Editor: Allan Girdler. 50¢ monthly. Buys all rights. Enclose S.A.S.E. for ms return. No sample copies available.

**Nonfiction:** "We are classified as a 'general' automotive magazine, and as such we take a wide-range view of the full automotive science as it relates to the knowledgeable consumer, hobbyist, and enthusiast. Our material is technically oriented, unexcelled in accuracy, and written to the highest standards of maturity, perceptivity, and style. We examine both the history and the newest frontiers in automotive technology; we report present developments and trends in design and performance; we dissect the machinery which is significant, and sometimes the men who make it so; and we continually point to better ways for the job to be done. All road tests and most auto industry evaluations are staff produced. However, we constantly seek new writing talent to produce such pieces as: 'Revenge of the Edsel' and 'The Pierce-Arrow That Never Got a Chance' (classic car). Also full length pieces for our 'Action Line' series: Good solid technical information supplemented by specific reader service how-to. 'How to Build a Buggy,' 'How to Cut Insurance Costs', 'Anti-Roll Bars,' 'Paint and Pray,' Average length is 2,000 to 3,000 words. Also occasional short articles (under 1,000 words) of historical or of a technically interesting nature. No set form or content. Query essential. Payment based on published length; minimum about $50 per page, including art."

**Photos:** Buys pix submitted with mss only. Uses b&w, 8x10 glossy or matte. Rarely buys color except on assignment basis. Most photography is used to illustrate articles.

**CHATELAINE,** 481 University Avenue, Toronto 2, Canada. Editor: Doris McCubbin Anderson. Managing Editor: Jean Y. Wright. Payment for all material is on acceptance. Chatelaine buys first world serial rights in English and French (the latter only to cover possible use in Chatelaine's sister French-language edition, edited in Montreal for French Canada). All manuscripts must be accompanied by a self-addressed, stamped envelope (international reply coupons in lieu of Canadian stamps if sent from outside Canada).

**Nonfiction:** Preferably submit a page or two outline-query first. Preferred full-length major pieces run from 2,000 to 3,600 words; a few shorter humorous or minor pieces from 1,000 up. Payment for an acceptable major article starts at $300. Subjects wanted are important national Canadian articles examining all and any facets of Canadian life especially as they concern or interest Canadian women. Examples: "Inside Ottawa," "Our New Abortion Law—Already Out-Dated?" and "The Thinking Woman's Diet," Nov. '69; "It's Family Christmas at the Fred Davises'" and "The Oslers Of Ontario," Dec. '69; "Why Are Canadians So Debt-Prone?" and "Nancy Greene— From Olympic Star to Happy Housewife," Jan. '70. Uses material on medical subjects; education. Also full-length personal experience stories with deep emotional impact. See, "My Son Smoked Marijuana," Oct. 1968. Subjects outside Canada need some Canadian tie-in. See "Chatelaine in Japan," Feb. '70. For all serious articles deep, accurate thorough research and rich detail is required. A shallow once-over-lightly treatment will not do for Chatelaine.

**Fiction:** Preferred length is 3,000 to 4,500 words, though this can vary depending on the story. No short shorts. Settings should be Canadian if at all possible. In demand are slick light romance; romantic or glamorous settings; down-to-earth recognizable human stories with real character impact. Also some adult fiction. Preferably, the central character should be a woman, involved in a situation with which Canadian women can identify and find recognizable. Very little demand for stories where the central character is a child (though children can be important secondary characters), or animal stories. Payment starts at $400. Send fiction manuscripts to Miss Almeda Glassey, Fiction Editor.

**CHILD LIFE,** 1100 Waterway Blvd., Indianapolis, Ind. 46202. Publisher: Beurt R. SerVaas; Editor: Rita Cooper; Managing

Editor: Beth W. Thomas. Published ten times yearly for children ages 7 to 12. Buys all rights unless otherwise specified by the author at time of submission. Reports in 8 to 10 weeks. Enclose S.A.S.E. with submissions. Will send editorial requirements sheet for Child Life and Children's Playmate on request. Deadlines six months prior to publication. Simultaneous submissions not accepted.

**Nonfiction:** 900 words maximum; present-day science, nature, general information, words, international stories. Little-known anecdotes about famous people, events or accomplishments in which identity is withheld until the end. See "Man of Words," Dec. 1968. Pays about 3¢ per word.

**Photos:** Picture stories on children, animals, events, nature, humor; any story that can be told better by pictures than in words. No isolated single photos wanted. Stories must have pace and progression. B&w glossy 8x10 preferred. Also buys photos submitted with mss to illustrate articles. Pays about $3 each.

**Fiction and Drama:** From 600 words for beginner stories to 900 for older children. Should be written in realistic, non-moralizing, non-academic style. Likes humor or suspense in fiction. No talking inanimate objects. See "Joey on Skates," Dec. 1968 for example of beginner story, and "Out of the Wilderness," Feb. 1969 for advanced story. Pays about 3¢ per word. Also very short, lively plays that can be produced in living room or classroom with minimum of simple props and small casts.

**Poetry:** Needs range from four-line couplets to long poems. Pays about 25¢ per line.

**Fillers:** Puzzles, mazes, tricks and games. See Rebus: "Open House-Molly Mouse," Dec. 1968.

**Make-its:** Should use materials readily available at home or school and involve a minimum of adult guidance. Explanatory sketches and/or a sample of the finished project should be included if practical.

**THE ELKS MAGAZINE,** 425 W. Diversey Parkway, Chicago, Ill. 60614. Articles Editor: J.A. Provost. Issued monthly for Elks and their families. Buys first North American rights. Pays on acceptance. Reports in 10 days. Editor will send sample copy on request. Enclose S.A.S.E.

**Nonfiction:** Anything of general interest, and of interest to the small businessman. Must be well-researched, well-organized, accurate and well-written—with a style that is lively but not flippant. Articles of interest to sportsmen, such as on hunting, golf, baseball, fishing, along with material related to holidays such as Christmas, Thanksgiving, etc. Preferred length: 2,000 to 2,500 words. Short articles, 1,000 words and up, are needed. Pays about 10¢ a word.

**Photos:** Buys photographs with mss. Pays $15. No color.

**Fiction:** Humor to 2,500 words is welcome.

**ELLERY QUEEN'S MYSTERY MAGAZINE,** 229 Park Avenue, South, New York, N.Y. 10003. All mss should be typed on one side of the paper and double-spaced. Please enclose S.A.S.E. in case ms must be returned; if outside the U.S., use International Postal Reply coupons for return postage. "Do not ask for criticism of stories; we receive too many submissions to make this possible." Pays on acceptance. Enclose S.A.S.E. for ms return.

**Fiction:** Crime, detective, suspense, all types of mystery stories are used—the psychological study, the deductive puzzle, the gamut from realism to fancy. Need tougher stories for the Black Mask section, but do not want sex, sadism or sensationalism for its own sake. "Three criteria: quality of writing, originality of plot, and craftsmanship. The most practical way to find out what EQMM wants is to read EQMM: nearly every issue will tell you all you need to know of our standards, and of our diversified approach." No query necessary. Would welcome detective and crime short stories with sports backgrounds —baseball, football, golf, auto racing, basketball, bowling, sky diving, yacht racing, scuba diving, even checkers—whatever sport writer is familiar with. Length: 4,000-6,000 words preferred, but stories of 10,000 and occasionally 20,000 words, short-shorts of 1,400-2,000 words also acceptable. Authors retain all subsidiary and supplementary rights, including TV, movies, etc. Rates for original stories 3¢-8¢ per word. Also looking for fine reprints—any type of crime, detective, or mystery story, no matter where it has been published before (providing the author owns and controls the reprint rights), and no matter how long ago the story first appeared. We pay special rates for reprints.

**ESSENCE,** (formerly Sapphire), 102 E. 30th St., New York, N.Y. 10016. Editor-in-Chief: Miss Ida Lewis. 60¢ monthly. Copyrighted. Circulation: 250,000. Will send a sample copy for 60¢. Aimed at Black women 18-34. Reports in four to six weeks. Buys North American serial rights only. Pays on acceptance. Mss should be typed, double-spaced, with return, stamped envelope enclosed.

**Nonfiction:** Wants general articles of interest to young or young-thinking Black women. No other particular requirements as to subject matter or style. 6,000 words maximum; also uses shorter pieces between 700-1,200 words. See "Black Man, Do You Love Me?" by Louise Meriwether, May, 1970 issue. Query preferred. Pays $150-$300 for short pieces; $300-$600 for longer articles.

**Photos:** Purchased both with mss and separately. Black themes. Portfolios must be seen by Art Director, Mr. John Gerbino, by appointment. Payment varies.

**Fiction:** Wants high quality stories of interest to Black women. No particular slants, taboos or subject matter. 2,500-3,000 words. No short-shorts. See "The Ride," by Audrey Lee, June, 1970 issue. Pays $300-$400. Address submissions to Sharyn S. Alexander, Fiction Editor.

**Poetry:** No limitations as to subject matter, style, etc. except high quality. Maximum length: 65 lines. Address to Sharyn S. Alexander, Poetry Editor.

**Fillers:** Newsbreaks and clippings containing little-known, current information of interest to the Black community. Payment varies.

**FARM JOURNAL,** Washington Square, Philadelphia, Penna. 19105. Editor: Lane Palmer. Monthly. Six separate editions printed, for the East, the Central States, Great Plains, the Southern, Southwest, and the Western parts of the U.S. Material bought for one or more editions depending upon where it fits. Payment made on acceptance and is the same regardless of editions in which the piece is used. Enclose S.A.S.E. for ms return.

**Nonfiction:** Timeliness and seasonality are very important. Material must be highly practical and should be helpful to as many farmers as possible. Farmers' experiences may apply to any phase of farming and animal raising, as well as to the farm home and the community. Queries always helpful. Technical material must be accurate. "The Farmer's Wife" section is open for homemaking experiences based on what a particular woman did. Allow a full three months for material in this department. Query before submitting material. Pays excellent rate.

**Photos:** Much in demand either separately or with short how-to material in picture stories and as illustrations for articles. Warm human interest pix for covers—activities on modern farms. For inside use, shots of home-made and handy ideas to get work done easier and faster, farm news photos, and pictures of children on the farm. In b&w, 8x10 glossies are preferred; color submissions should be 2¼x2¼ for the cover, and 35mm for inside use. Pays $50 and up for b&w shot; $75 and up for color.

**FIELD AND STREAM,** 383 Madison Ave., New York, N.Y. 10017. Editor: Clare Conley. Issued monthly at 50¢ a copy. $5 a year. Reports within three weeks. Buys first rights. Query first. Holt Rinehart & Winston also publish Special Interest Publications which include several annual Field and Stream guides and handbooks on outdoor recreation and sports. Editor: Kenneth Anderson. These guides use freelance articles and photos; query required. Enclose S.A.S.E. with submissions and queries.

**Nonfiction:** This is a broad-based outdoor service magazine. Editorial content ranges from very basic how-to stories that tell either in pictures or words how an outdoor technique is done or device made. Articles of penetrating depth about national conservation, game management, resource management, and recreation development problems. Hunting, fishing, camping, travel, nature, photography, equipment, flying, skin diving, snowmobiling, cooking, workshop, and other activities allied to the outdoors. If an article doesn't contain plenty of helpful information that is either new or has a new slant, it won't make the grade here. The "me and Joe" story is about dead, with the exception of adventure articles. However, service articles should have their information sugar-coated with a liberal use of short illuminating anecdotes. With the exception of Canada and Mexico, much foreign material is staff written. Both where-to and how-to articles should be well illustrated. Prefers color to b&w. Submit outline first with photos. Length, 2,500 words. Payment varies depending upon the name of the author, quality of work, importance of the article. Pays 12¢ per word and up. Usually buys pix with mss.

**Photos:** With mss, see nonfiction. When purchased separately, pays $25 for b&w; $50 and up for color. Uses photo stories on all above-listed subjects plus boating.

**Fillers:** Occasionally buys fillers of 500 to 1,000 words. Must be unusual or helpful subjects.

**THE FURROW,** Deere & Co., John Deere Rd., Moline, Ill. 61265. Editor: Ralph E. Reynolds. Free, 8-12 times yearly, for upper income farm families. Will send free sample copy to a writer on request. Reports on submissions in two weeks. Buys international rights. Pays on acceptance. Include S.A.S.E. for ms return.

**Nonfiction:** Occasionally purchases ideas or makes article assignments; pays about 10¢ per word. Uses short articles, up to 1,500 words, aimed specifically at upper-income farm audience. Style should be friendly and conversational but dignified. Human and socio-economic features must be genuinely rural—no struggling for farm slant. Query first.

**Photos:** Purchased with mss. Pays $10-$15 for 8x10 glossies; prefers color negatives to transparencies; 35 mm slides are accepted.

**GOOD HOUSEKEEPING,** 959 Eighth Ave., New York, N.Y. 10019. Editor: Wade H. Nichols. Issued monthly; 50¢ per copy. Enclose S.A.S.E. for return of queries and submissions.

**Nonfiction:** Elizabeth Frank, Articles Editor; Robert Liles, Features Editor; Norris Randolf, Editor for "The Better Way." Three categories for nonfiction: 1. General articles on subjects of topicality and consequence that concern readers in a meaningful way. This might be anything from a report on a current controversial problem or a vexing social issue to a dramatic personal narrative dealing with unusual experiences of average families. Most writers miss the boat because of lack of impact, warmth and dramatic appeal with which the average housewife can identify. Material must be accurate, honest, bright, comprehensive and imaginatively presented. Depth reporting is a must. Most articles run between 3,000 and 5,000 words. Query with an informal letter first. Outlines must pinpoint the idea specifically. Rates range from $500 for short pieces to $5,000 for important features. 2. Short features include small pieces on big celebrities. These miniatures never attempt to tell everything about anyone, but try to explore some single and interesting angle of the subject's life or point of view. Prefer subjects whose names are well established. Also interested in short humorous essay. 3. Material for "The Better Way": This is the special information section of the magazine. Since it must fit a stylized format, they don't buy a finished article—just ideas and, on occasion, depth research on a subject of practical interest to housewives. Pays $25 to $50 for ideas and up to $250 for research assignments.

**Fiction:** Naome Lewis, Fiction Editor. Must portray problems which offer a strong element of reader identification. Characterization and thought content count more than plot, but also look for stories which contain practical and believable solutions offered in dramatic contexts. Average length is 4,000 words. Novelettes, book excerpts, condensations and serials also used. Payment starts at $1,000.

**Poetry:** Usually overstocked in light verse category. Address serious poetry (preferably short) to Leonhard Dowty. Pays $25 and up for verse on basis of $5 a line.

**Fillers:** Submit to Robert Liles. Humorous short-short prose for "Light Housekeeping" feature needed. Payment $25 to $100. Buys epigrams, short humor.

**GRIT,** Williamsport, Pa. 17701. Editor: Kenneth D. Rhone; Feature Editor: Terry L. Ziegler. 20¢ weekly for small town family audience. Buys one-time rights. Pays on acceptance. Does not buy fiction from freelancers. Enclose S.A.S.E.

**Nonfiction:** Human interest, inspirational articles; anything interesting to small town audience. Length: 300 to 750 words. Payment varies according to length, quality, etc.

**Photos:** Purchased with mss or captions only. 8x10 prints preferred; some editorial color used. (Transparencies of professional quality required.) Payment varies.

**Poetry:** Send to Helen Matthews.

**GUIDEPOSTS MAGAZINE,** 3 W. 29th St., New York, N.Y. 10001. Executive Editor: Leonard E. LeSourd. Guideposts is an inspirational monthly magazine for all faiths in which men and women from all walks of life tell how they overcame obstacles, rose above failures, met sorrow, learned to conquer themselves, and became more effective people through the direct application of the religious principles by which they live. Buys first rights. Enclose S.A.S.E.

**Nonfiction and Fillers:** Articles and features should be written in simple, anecdotal style with an emphasis on human interest. Short features up to approximately 250 words ($10-$25) would be considered for such Guideposts features as: "Calendar of Holidays and Holy Days," "Fragile Moments," and other short items which appear at the end of major articles. Short mss of approximately 250-500 words ($25-$50) would be considered for such features as "Quiet People" and general one-page stories. Full-length mss, 500-1,500 words ($50-$100). All mss should be typed, double-spaced and accompanied by a stamped self-addressed envelope. Inspirational newspaper or magazine clippings often form the basis of articles in Guideposts, but it is unable to pay for material of this type and will not return clippings unless the sender specifically asks and encloses postage for return.

**HIGHLIGHTS FOR CHILDREN,** 803 Church St., Honesdale, Pa. 18431. Editor-In-Chief: Dr. Garry Cleveland Myers. Published monthly except June-July and August-September combined issues and two issues in February. For children two to 12. No poetry. Multiple submission discouraged. Buys all rights. Pays on acceptance. Reports within two months. Query not required, but acceptable. Enclose S.A.S.E. for ms return.

**Nonfiction:** Most factual features, including history and science, are written on assignment by persons with rich background and mastery in their respective fields. But contributions always welcomed from new writers, especially science teachers, engineers, scientists, historians, etc., who can interpret to children useful, interesting, and authentic facts, but not of the bizarre or "Ripley" type; also writers who have lived abroad and can interpret well the ways of life, especially of children in other countries, and who don't leave the impression that our ways are always the best. Query not necessary. Exceptional science articles within 1,000 words bring from $50 to $150; other factual articles up to $100. Needs some factual articles 400 to 500 words in length and some 800 to 1,000 words, written by persons with background, persons who know. Direct, simple style, interesting content, without word embellishment; not rewritten from encyclopedias. Avoid suggestions of material reward for upward striving, suggestions of war, crime and violence. See "Elizabeth Keckley," by Mabelle E. Martin, Feb. '70. Pays from $75 to $100.

**Fiction:** Unusual, wholesome stories of 400 to 500 words in length and some 800 to 1,000 words in length, appealing to both girls and boys. Vivid, full of action and word-pictures, easy to illustrate. Seeks stories that the child 8 to 12 will eagerly read, and the child 2 to 6 will like to hear when read to him. "We print no stories just to be read aloud; they must serve a two-fold purpose. We encourage authors not to hold themselves to controlled word lists. Right now we need stories not over 500 words which the child from 6 to 8 may read. Especially need humorous stories, but also need winter stories; urban stories; horse stories; and especially some mystery stories void of violence; and stories introducing characters from different ethnic groups; holiday stories devoid of Santa Claus and the Easter Bunny. Avoid suggestion of material reward for upward striving. Moral teaching should be subtle. War, crime and violence are taboo. Some fanciful stories wanted. Examples of what children like are: "Holes for Sale," by Barbara Bartocci in the March, 1969 issue, "Little No Name," by Laura Arlon in the February, 1969 issue, "Adventure of the Footprints," by Elizabeth Rainbow, Feb. '70. Payment is 5¢ to 15¢ a word.

**Fillers:** Activities: Original party plans for children 7 to 12, clearly described in 600 to 800 words, including pencil drawings or samples of items to be illustrated. Pays $30 to $100. Also novel but tested ideas in arts and crafts, with clear directions, easily illustrated, preferably with made-up models. Projects must require only salvage material or inexpensive easy-too-obtain material. Especially desirable if easy enough for early primary grades and appropriate to special seasons and days. Pays $10 to $50. Also finger plays with lots of action, easy for very young children to grasp and for parents to dramatize, step-by-step, with hands and fingers. Avoid wordiness. Pays up to $50 on acceptance. Also uses some puzzles but none which require that the child write in the book.

**MARRIAGE, THE MAGAZINE FOR HUSBAND AND WIFE,** St. Meinrad, Ind. 47577. Editor: Brian F. Daly. 50¢ monthly. Circulation: 63,000. Will send sample copy to a writer for 10¢ Reports on submissions in two weeks. Buys North American serial rights only. Pays on acceptance. Enclose S.A.S.E. for ms return.

**Nonfiction:** Uses five different types of articles: (1) Informative and inspirational articles on all aspects of marriage, especially husband and wife relationship. Length: 2,000-2,500 words. (2) Personal essays relating dramatic or amusing incidents that point up the human side of marriage. Up to 1,500 words in length. (3) Profiles of outstanding couples or couples whose story will be of interest for some special reason, and profiles of individuals who contribute to the betterment of marriage. Length: 1,500-2,000 words. (4) Interviews with authorities in the fields of marriage (on current problems and new developments). Length: Up to 2,000 words. Pays 5¢ per word. (5) "We Tried This"—short, personal accounts telling about original solutions to husband and wife problems. Length: up to 400 words. Pays $15. "At Our House"—short, personal accounts of unusual or amusing incidents of family living. Length: Up to 400 words; pays $15. Query not necessary.

**Photos:** Singles. Illustrated articles in b&w. Pays $25. Requires model releases. Department Editor: O.E. Mansfield.

**Fiction:** Short-shorts up to 1,000 words; short stories 2,000-3,000 words in length. Should deal with husband-wife theme: Pays 5¢ per word.

**Poetry:** Subject matter same as above (see Fiction).

**Fillers:** Up to 400 words.

**MATURE YEARS,** 201 8th Ave. South, Nashville, Tenn. 37202. Editor: Daisy D. Warren. Issued quarterly for persons 60 years of age and above. Reports on submissions in 2 months. Buys all rights. Pays on acceptance. Will send sample copy to writer for 35¢ Include S.A.S.E. for ms return. Christmas and Thanksgiving deadlines are roughly 15 months before the issue appears in final form.

**Nonfiction:** Articles on ways older adults have organized to help in community service projects or on unique ways individuals and groups are meeting older citizens' needs. Pays 3¢ per word. See "The Meaning of PAL" by Carl H. Holden, June-August, '70. 1,200-1,500 words.

**Photos:** Above-average quality 8x10 b&w glossies which illustrate mss are purchased separately. Payments vary from $7-$20 each, according to quality, etc.

**Fiction:** Same length as nonfiction. Pays 4¢ per word. Not interested in personal anecdotes, saccharine or overly sentimental stories.

**Poetry:** Pays $1 per line.

**Fillers:** Puzzles, short humor.

**OUTDOOR LIFE,** 355 Lexington Ave., New York, N.Y. 10017. Editor: William E. Rae. Issued monthly; 50¢ a copy; $5 a year. No fiction. Enclose self-addressed, stamped envelope for return of queries and submissions.

**Nonfiction:** Essentially a hunting and fishing magazine. Much true adventure is used along with how-to stories, new techniques in hunting and fishing, etc.; 3,000 to 4,000 words. Also uses similar stories on woodcraft, camping, firearms, motorboats and tackle. Writers should develop local atmosphere of a story, describe the country where they hunt and fish, the people and customs they may encounter. Narrative approach preferred. Story should show how another hunter or fisherman can enjoy a similar experience. Pays top rates, starting at $350 for a full-length piece, on acceptance. Query first.

**Photos:** Most material should be illustrated with good photographs. Also uses picture stories of from four to six pages. Uses both b&w and color photos. Color submissions must be transparencies. Uses 35 mm and up.

**OUTDOOR WORLD,** 1645 Tullie Circle, N.E., Atlanta, Ga. 30329. Editor: Ernest S. Booth. Bimonthly. $1.25 a copy. Copyrighted. For the outdoorsman and the individual who appreciates nature. Aimed at individuals whose outdoor reading interests lie somewhere between hunting and fishing magazines and magazines more technically slanted. Reports within four weeks. Usually buys North American serial rights. Pays on acceptance. Include S.A.S.E. for ms return.

**Nonfiction:** "Plants, animals, fossils, rocks, stars, oceans, etc.; travel, camping, mountain climbing, skiing, boating, outdoor recreation other than commercial sports; places of interest (national parks, refuges, forests and monuments), deserts, mountains, rivers, islands. Needs more human interest articles with people involved in outdoor activities related to nature and wilderness appreciation. Writing must be crisp and clear, moving toward a climax. Mediocre or slapdash writing and heavy, academic prose taboo. Statements of fact not easy to substantiate must be documented." No hunting or fishing pieces. Lead articles 1,200 to 2,500 words. Short pieces about 500 words. Pays about $125 for major articles, but something new and significant, or exclusive, is worth considering more. Query preferred. Address Dorothy Deer, Editor.

**Photos:** Preferably purchased with ms. Some single photos and photo series. Nature and the outdoors, including outdoor recreational activities. Color—prefers large format transparencies, but sharp 35mm acceptable. Pays $30 to $100. 8x10 b&w glossies bring $10 to $25. Ray Simons, Editor.

**Poetry:** Dealing with nature, or as above for nonfiction. Esthetic appeal.

**Fillers:** Puzzles, short humor. Approximately 250 words. Pays $10 to $15. Deadlines six months prior to date of issue.

**PLAYBOY,** 919 N. Michigan, Chicago, Ill. 60603. Editor-Publisher: Hugh M. Hefner; Exec. Editor: Michael Demarest. Managing Editor: Jack J. Kessie. $1 monthly. Reports in two weeks. Buys first rights and others. Enclose S.A.S.E. with mss and queries.

**Nonfiction:** "Articles should be carefully researched and written with wit and insight; a lucid style is important. Little true adventure or how-to material. Check magazine for subject matter. Pieces on jazz, outstanding contemporary men, sports, politics, sociology, business and finance, games, all areas of interest to the urban male." A query is advisable here. Length is about 5,000-7,000 words. Pays $3,000 for lead article; $2,000 regular. The Playboy interviews run between 8,000 and 12,000 words.

The freelancer outlines the questions and the Editorial staff may add a few of its own. For an example of what is wanted, see "Playboy Interview: Jesse Jackson" in the Nov. '69 issue. Pays $2,000. Runs an interview 10 times a year, a panel discussion twice a year. The panel discussion is a conversation of seven to ten people speaking on a subject of topical interest. 8,000-12,000 words. Pays $4,000. Has a movie reviewer, record reviewer, theater critic, book reviewers, food and drink columnist; not looking for material in these areas. Authors who grant Playboy first refusal on their work will be eligible to receive a rising scale of payment for each work purchased. The basic payment scale detailed above will apply to the first purchase. The price for each additional purchase of standard-length material will increase in increments of $100 each, to a maximum purchase price of $4,000 for lead material and $3,000 for non-lead material. The price for each purchase of short-short material will be equal to one-half the price of a standard-length, non-lead piece, with a maximum purchase price of $1,500. Also pays $50-$250 for idea. Pays more for idea with research which is assigned to a staff writer. If a commissioned article does not meet standards, will pay a turndown price of $400.

**Photos:** Vincent T. Tajiri, Picture Editor, suggests that all photographers interested in contributing make a thorough study of the photography currently appearing in the magazine. Generally, all assignments are carefully controlled and handled by staff and contributing photographers working out of Playboy's full-time studios in Chicago and Los Angeles. Qualified freelancers are encouraged to submit samples, since Playboy—despite an established list of photographers to whom assignments are given—is in search of new talent and ideas. All assignments are on an "all rights" basis with payments scaled from $600 per color page; $300 per b&w; cover, $850. Playmate photography for entire shooting, $5,000. Assignments and submissions handled by Bev Chamberlain, Associate Picture Editor. Assignments generally made on minimum guarantee basis. Film and processing expenses plus other expenses honored on assignments.

**Fiction:** Both light and serious fiction. Entertainment pieces are clever, smoothly-written stories. Serious fiction must come up to the best contemporary standards in substance, idea, and style. Both, however, should be designed to appeal to the edu-cated, well-informed male reader. General types include comedy, mystery, fantasy, horror, science-fiction, adventure, social-realism, "problem," and psychological stories. One special re-quirement for science-fiction is that it deal—in fresh and origi-nal ways—with human dilemmas more than technological problems. Fiction on controversial topics is welcome; the only taboo is against formless sketches and excessively subjective writing. Playboy has serialized novels by Ian Fleming, Vladi-mir Nabokov, Len Deighton, and Evan Hunter. Other fiction contributors include Saul Bellow, John Cheever, Bernard Mala-mud, and P.G. Wodehouse. Fiction lengths are from 2,000-10,000 words; occasionally short-shorts of 1,000-1,500 words are used. Pays $3,000 for lead story; $2,000 regular; $1,000 short-short. Rates rise for additional acceptances. Rate for Ri-bald Classics is $400. Unsolicited mss must be accompanied by stamped, self-addressed envelope. Robie Macauley, Fiction Editor.

**Fillers:** Party Jokes are always welcome. Pays $50 each. Also in-teresting items for Playboy After Hours, front section (best to check this carefully before submission). Here, pays anywhere from $50 for a two-line typographical error to $250 for an orig-inal lead item. Subject matter should be humorous, ironic. Pre-fers lengths of 20 to 500 words.

**THE PROGRESSIVE FARMER,** 821 North 19th St., Birming-ham, Ala. 35202. 25¢ single copy price. Will send sample copy to a writer for 40¢ Reports on submissions in one month. Buys first publication rights. Enclose S.A.S.E. for ms return.

**Nonfiction:** Articles about the activities of Southern farm home-makers. Submit to Oris Cantrell, Women's Editor. Articles deal-ing with personal experiences in farming; how-to-do-it articles. Wants easy-to-read, farm-oriented writing. Send to Joe A. El-liott,. Editorial Director. Regular columns: "Handy Devices" (farm), "Jokes." Query essential. Pays $15 per column and up.

**Photos:** Purchased with mss; b&w, 8x10. Pays $5-$10 per photo.

**Fiction:** Farm-slanted stories. Send to Eugene Butler, The Pro-gressive Farmer, 3612 Noble Ave., Dallas, Texas.

**Poetry:** Farm-slanted verse, 4 to 12 lines. Submit to Oris Can-trell, Women's Editor. Payment varies.

**READER'S DIGEST,** Pleasantville, N.Y. 10570. Issued monthly; monthly; 50¢ a copy. Items intended for a particular feature should be directed to the editor in charge of that feature, although the contribution may later be referred to another section of the magazine as seeming more suitable.

**Nonfiction:** Reader's Digest is especially interested in receiving the following sorts of material: First Person Articles. An article for this series must be a previously unpublished narrative of an unusual personal experience. It may be dramatic, inspirational or humorous, but it must have a quality of narrative and interest comparable to stories published in this series. Contributions must be typewritten, preferably double-spaced, no longer than 2,500 words. It is requested that documents or photographs not be sent. Manuscripts cannot be acknowledged, and will be returned—usually within eight or ten weeks—only when return postage accompanies them. Address to: First Person Editor. Payment rate on acceptance: $3,000. Base rate for general articles is $2,000 for first sale.

**Fillers:** Life in These United States contributions must be true, unpublished stories from one's own experience, revelatory of adult human nature, and providing appealing or humorous sidelights on the American scene. Maximum length: 300 words. Address to: Life in U.S. Editor. Payment rate on publication: $200. Humor in Uniform: True and unpublished stories based on experiences in the armed forces. Maximum length: 300 words. Address: Humor in Uniform Editor. Payment rate on publication: $200. Campus Comedy: True unpublished stories about life at college. Maximum length: 300 words. Payment rate on publication: $200. Toward More Picturesque Speech: The first contributor of each item used in this department is paid $25. Contributions should be dated, and the sources must be given. Address: Picturesque Speech Editor. Current issues carry notes about requirements in the following departments: Personal Glimpses, Laughter, the Best Medicine, and other brief items.

**REDBOOK MAGAZINE,** 230 Park Ave., New York, N.Y. 10017. Issued monthly; 50¢ a copy; $3 a year. 75-80% freelance. Buys first North American rights. Reports in 2-3 weeks. Pays top rates, on acceptance. Enclose S.A.S.E.

**Nonfiction:** Robert J. Levin, Articles Editor. Narratives (see "The Court Martial of Susan Schnall" in Nov. 1969 issue) and exploratory factual pieces (see "The Battle Against Sex Education" in Sept. 1969 issue) are always wanted; conditions which affect the magazine's readers, who are young married women in the 18 to 34-year-old group, and about which they can do something. See "What Doctors Now Know About Your Unborn Baby," February 1969 issue. Inspiration pieces are welcome if they are written from the point of view of an individual or family. Also interested in submissions for "Young Mother's Story" feature. "If you have had some experience in your family, social or marital life that you feel may be particularly interesting and helpful to other mothers, we would be interested in seeing your story. Please don't hestiate to send it because you think your spelling or punctuation may be a bit rusty; we don't judge these stories on the basis of technicalities and we do make minor editing changes. For each 1,000 to 2,000 words accepted for publication, we pay $500. Mss, accompanied by a stamped, self-addressed envelope, must be signed (although name will be withheld on request), and mailed to: Young Mother's Story, c/o Redbook Magazine. Stories do not have to by typed; of course we appreciate it when they are legibly written." For articles, preferred length, 4,000-5,000 words; shorts down to 2,000 words.

**Fiction:** Mrs. Neal G. Thorpe, Fiction Editor. Uses a great variety of types of fiction, with contemporary stories appealing especially to women in demand. Short stories of 3,500 to 5,000 words are always needed. Also short-shorts of 1,400-1,600 words. Short-shorts begin at $750. Short stories begin at $1,000. The editors want more and better complete novels of 40,000 words.

**SATURDAY REVIEW,** 380 Madison Ave., New York, N.Y. 10017. Editor: Norman Cousins. Weekly at 50¢ per copy, $9 per year. Most articles and all book reviews are assigned, but freelance material is carefully considered. Pays on publication. Reports as soon as possible. Enclose S.A.S.E.

**Nonfiction:** High literary quality is essential. First-rate articles on international affairs, politics, art, education, science, music, movies, theater and communications (the press, TV, advertising, etc.). Emphasis is on seasoned opinions and judgements backed by solid facts. Payment for articles averages between $300 and $600. Query suggested.

**Photos:** Uses 8x10 glossy photos and buys one-time rights for these.

**Poetry:** Uses high literary quality verse.

**Fillers:** Short humor. Also occasional 900-word guest editorials. Solid reputation is invariably necessary to back up opinions.

**SOUTH AND WEST,** 2601 S. Phoenix, Ft. Smith, Ark. 72901. Editor: Sue Abbott Boyd. $1 quarterly. Will send sample copy to a writer for 75¢ Reports on submissions within 2 weeks. Buys North American serial rights only. Include S.A.S.E. for all mss and queries.

**Nonfiction:** Appropriate feature articles concerning poetry will also be included from time to time. Also includes some book reviews.

**Poetry:** The purpose of this magazine is to encourage new poets as well as give voice to those already established. Emphasis is on modern poetry, expression of new and young thought. "We prefer work that is individualistic, that reflects the personality of the writer." Length: preferably under 37 lines, but will not reject good long poem. All types of poems receive equal consideration. Payment in contributor's copy; substantial awards.

**SOUTHERN SCENE,** Public Relations Dept., Southern Airways, Inc., Atlanta Airport, Atlanta, Ga. 30320. Editor: Redmond Tyler. Published quarterly. Free to Southern Airways passengers; aimed at male travelers. Copyrighted. 75% freelance. Will send free sample copy on request. Reports usually within two weeks. Rights purchased vary. Enclose S.A.S.E. Pays on acceptance.

**Nonfiction:** High quality and of interest to a well-educated audience (66% of whom have college degrees); about the South, New York or Chicago, or about travel, business, food and drink with a Southern slant. No race articles per se, but welcomes articles about all races. 2,000-4,000 words. Query suggested. Pays between $200-$400 depending upon subject and accompanying photos.

**Photos:** Purchased with mss or with captions only. Same subject matter as nonfiction. Pay varies from approx. $50 min. to $200 for photo assignment.

**THREE/FOUR,** 201 Eighth Ave., S., Nashville, Tenn. 37203. Editor: Betty M. Buerki. Issued monthly in weekly parts for third and fourth graders. Will send free sample copy to a writer on request. Reports in one to two months. Prefers to buy all rights. Pays on acceptance. Enclose S.A.S.E. for ms return. United Methodist church. Copyrighted.

**Nonfiction:** Desires articles about science, nature, animals, customs in other countries, and other subjects of interest to readers. Length: approximately 500 words. Pays 4¢ a word. Deadlines are one year ahead of publication date.

**Photos:** Usually purchased with manuscripts only. Also uses photo features. Prefers 8x10 glossies.

**Fiction:** Historical stories should be true to their setting. Stories which make a point about values should not sound moralistic. Also accepts stories written just for fun. Length: 500 to 1,000 words. Writers must know children. Fictionalized Bible stories must be based upon careful research. Pays 4¢ a word.

**Poetry:** Accepts light verse or religious verse. Pays 50¢ to $1 per line.

**Fillers:** Puzzles, quizzes, and matching games.

**TODAY'S HEALTH,** 535 N. Dearborn St., Chicago, Ill. 60610. Editor: Bryon T. Scott. 60¢ monthly. Will send free sample copy to writer on request. Accepting no unsolicited mss or poetry; query first. Reports in one week on queries, two to three weeks on mss. Buys all rights. Pays on acceptance. Enclose S.A.S.E. with queries and submissions.

**Nonfiction:** Uses sound articles on any subject related to health, including pictorials, world of medicine and research with emphasis on contemporary issues. Prefers a positive approach, telling readers what they can do to preserve their health. Likes clear, thorough, concise writing. Material must be understandable to young adults who have little or no science training. Typical readers are parents of school-age children. Must be scientifically sound, authoritative; no "my operation" articles. Authority for most statements in articles should come from M.D.'s. Lengths, 1,000 to 2,500 words, but no rigid limits. Average payment for full length piece is $600. Query first. For examples, see "Sensitivity Training: Fad, Fraud, or New Frontier." "Race to Reclaim a Dead Man's Eyes," "'Predictable' Hazards of Childhood," and "Skeezer: The Canine Child Therapist," in the Jan. '70 issue.

**Photos:** Cover color transparencies 2¼x2¼ or larger; pays $200. Photos to illustrate regular text usually assigned. Model releases required for cover photos. Buys first-time rights. If photographer works on assignment for daily rate, publication retains all rights to photos.

**TRUE CONFESSIONS,** 205 E. 42nd St., New York, N.Y. 10017. Editor: Florence J. Moriarty. 50¢ monthly. Reports on submissions in 4 weeks. Buys all rights. Pays on acceptance. Enclose S.A.S.E. for ms return.

**Nonfiction:** Limited market for fresh, well-written, solid features dealing with love and marriage problems. Length: 2,000-4,000 words. Child-care features covering problems of infancy to toddler stage. Length: 500-1,200 words. Query Helen Vincent, Managing Editor, with outline of features. Must have fresh slant, interest-holding development of material. Pays 5¢ per word for features, but rate varies according to merit.

**Fiction:** Strongly realistic, emotional, exciting, woman-oriented first-person stories about average people who make highly interesting reading. "We are after the unusual that is also believable. Our greatest need is for stories in the 5,000-7,500 word class. All stories must be based on themes and problem situations that relate and are of interest to young women. Special attention should be given the handling of a story's lead. It must be provocative, immediately stirring up reader interest for the story that is about to unfold. The characters should come through as real people, not puppets who are manipulated by the writer to 'make the story come out right'." No abnormal sex or strictly sex-situation stories wanted. Pays 5¢ per word. Uses novelettes, about 18,000 words. For a story to command this length, it must have adequate plot complication and strong drama. Uses one book-length novelette an issue; pays flat rate of $800.

**Fillers:** Brief provocative material suitable to format; see Nonfiction above.

**YOUNG EXPLORERS,** Concordia Children's Newspapers, 3558 S. Jefferson Ave., St. Louis, Mo. 63118. Issued weekly by the Lutheran Church–Missouri Synod for children in grades three and four, ages eight and nine. 34¢ each quarter in bulk; $1.75 a year for single copies. Reports on submissions in two to three weeks. Will send a free sample copy to a writer on request. Pays on acceptance. Address all material to Managing Editor. Enclose S.A.S.E. for ms return.

**Nonfiction:** News of the Christian church as it relates to the lives of the children of this age level. "The objectives of the publication include the development of a concept of and an appreciation for the place and function of the Christian church in the world today at the readers' level of emotional and spiritual maturity." Feature stories which appeal to the experiences and interests of eight and nine year olds. Pays $3 to $10 for 200 to 500 words.

**Photos:** Should appeal to the 8-9 year olds. B&w, 8x10 preferred. Pays $2.50 to $7.50.

**Poetry:** Occasionally purchases poems for eight and nine year olds. Pays $2.

**Fillers:** Appropriate humor, and puzzles which have a religious theme.

# Trade Journals

**AMERICAN LAUNDRY DIGEST,** 500 N. Dearborn St., Chicago, Ill. 60610. Editor: Earl Fischer. Monthly to management of all types of laundries: family service, industrial, linen supply, diaper service, coinop and institutional. Pays on publication. Buys first rights. Will send free sample copy on request. Reports promptly on submissions. Enclose S.A.S.E.

**Nonfiction:** No length limits. Plant stories or pure interviews with stress on marketing, related to timely developments in textiles, production, labor or society. Stress applies even to nonprofit institutional operations which must be competitive with outside service firms. Cannot name manufacturers or their products but must get specifics generically. Payment negotiable. Minimum of 3¢ per word. Editor says, "Be concise, human, controversial. Probe for whys and why nots, exhausting every possible option in line of questioning. Attribute quotes in present tense; keep informal flavor with depth of thought. Avoid glowing praise. Report the bad with the good—what you see, as you see it, as well as what you're told, even if words and actions are inconsistent."

**Photos:** Purchased with mss or with captions only. Candid action shots. Prefers 8x10 b&w glossy; 5x7 usually okay for close-ups. Pays $5.

**Fillers:** Ten to 300 words. Pays $3 and up. Newsbreaks, clippings.

**APPLIANCE SERVICE NEWS,** 5841 W. Montrose Ave., Chicago, Ill. 60634. Editor and Publisher: J.J. Charous. 35¢ monthly to firms and technicians which install and service electric and gas home appliances: laundry equipment, ranges, refrigerators, dishwashers, vacuum cleaners and other portable appliances, etc. Reports on submissions within 30 days. Buys all rights. Pays on publication. Will not return material unless accompanied by S.A.S.E.

**Nonfiction:** Feature articles on everything related to appliance service; including success stories with photos, methods of business operation. Also technical articles on portable and major appliances, both gas and electric, and refrigeration. Writer's guide information available. Length: up to 2,500 words. Pays 3¢-5¢ per word for feature-length pieces with photos.
**Photos:** Glossies purchased with mss or with captions only. Pays $5-$10. Also $5 for photo-caption cutline stories.
**Fillers:** News shorts about new business openings, expansions, unusual experiences to exclude manufacturers. No clippings wanted. Pays 3¢-5¢ per word.

**BUTANE-PROPANE NEWS,** P. O. Box 3027, Arcadia, Calif. 91006. Editor-Publisher: William W. Clark. Issued monthly for LP-gas distributor dealers with bulk storage plants, LP bottled gas dealers and manufacturers of appliances and equipment. Will send free sample copy on request. Reports on submissions within one week. Buys all rights. Pays on publication. Enclose S.A.S.E. for ms return.
**Nonfiction:** Articles on advertising and promotional programs; plant design, marketing operating techniques and policies; management problems; new, unusual or large usages of LP-gas. Completeness of coverage, reporting in depth, emphasis on the why and the how are musts. "Brevity essential but particular angles should be covered pretty thoroughly." Queries preferred to submission on speculation. Pays 3¢ per word or $30 per page.
**Photos:** Purchased with mss. 8x10 desired but not required; can work from negatives. Pays $5.
**Fillers:** Clippings and newsbreaks pertinent to LPG industry. Clippings regarding competitive fuels (electricity, oil) with relationship that would have impact on LPG industry.

**CANADIAN GROCER,** 481 University Ave., Toronto 2, Ont. Canada. Editor: F.M. Shore. Published monthly, 3rd of each month. $1 a copy. Pays on acceptance. Reports in two weeks. Buys first rights. Sample copy will be sent on request. Enclose S.A.E. and Int'l Reply coupons.
**Nonfiction and Photos:** Articles, 500 to 1,000 words long, with one to four clear pictures, well-captioned, on solving merchandising problems. Query first. Needs correspondents from some

regions of Canada, so a Canadian writer should query first to learn if his region is covered. Primarily interested in Canadian food distribution news and merchandising articles. 5¢ a word for features. 75¢ an inch for news. $5 a pic.

**NATIONAL FISHERMAN,** (including Maine Coast Fisherman and Pacific Fisherman), Camden, Me. 04843. Editor: David R. Getchell. 50¢ monthly for commercial fishing and boat building readership. Will send free sample copy to a writer on request. Reports on submissions in 1-2 weeks. Buys one-time rights. Publication not copyrighted. Enclose S.A.S.E. for ms return.

**Nonfiction:** Features and articles pertaining to commercial fishing, boat building and general marine subjects. Prefers informal style, human interest, unpretentious approach. Length: up to 3,000 words. Some technical detail necessary in certain stories; helpful data sheets available. Pays 50¢ per column inch on acceptance; price for text and photo package somewhat above regular rate. Article proposals should be accompanied by sample of work.

**Photos:** Purchased with mss or with captions. Good quailty, size varies. Prefers 5x7 or 8x10 b&w; can use b&w snapshots. Pays $3-$5.

**Fillers:** Long or short news items pertaining to commercial fishing, boat building and general marine subjects. Pay 50¢ per column inch on publication.

**RENT-ALL,** 8 John St., Southport, Conn. 06490. Editor: Joseph R. Nutt. Free monthly for rental equipment operators. Circulation: 10,000. Will send free sample copy to a writer on request. Reports on submissions vary. Buys all rights. Pays on publication. Enclose S.A.S.E. for ms return.

**Nonfiction:** "Articles on any rental items; especially stories dealing with unusual and/or unique items or procedures of interest to a majority of our readers. Pix that tell a story preferred. Word length should not exceed 1,500." Query first with brief outline. Pays 5¢ per word, with approved query; 3¢ per word, unsolicited; extra for photos. Query editor about special issues.

**Photos:** Purchased with mss; see above (Nonfiction). B&w, 8x10 or 5x7. Pays $5.

**Fillers:** Newsbreaks, short humor pertaining to rental equipment industry. RenTip column features short (150 words) tips for rental operators on better methods of storage, display, renting, etc. Pays $10 each (with one photo).

**THE VOLUNTARY AND COOPERATIVE GROUPS MAGA-ZINE,** 360 N. Michigan, Chicago, Ill. 60601. Editor and Publisher: Richard W. Mulville. Issued monthly; $1 a copy; $15 a year. Reports in about 2 weeks. Buys exclusive rights in the field. Will send a sample copy on request. Enclose S.A.S.E. for return of all submissions.
**Nonfiction and Photos:** Contents touch on all aspects of food warehousing and the retailer services provided by warehouses, with articles originating at the warehouse. Retail operations are discussed as they are related to warehouse activities. Some articles may be written from the retailer point of view, but only when they deal with an outstanding retailer operation, and even then they eventually include a tie-in to the warehousing servicing that retailer. Articles usually fit under one of the following department titles: buying, advertising/merchandising, retail development, materials handling, transportation, perishables, non-foods, management, plant development, data processing. Should be written in a "nuts-and-bolts" style. Meaningful facts and figures make up large part of copy. Only one or two photos or illustrations are normally used. Pays $25-$35 per printed page including pix, on publication. All articles must have approval of organization supplying the facts before submission.

**WESTERN LUMBER AND BUILDING MATERIALS MER-CHANT,** (formerly California Lumber Merchant), 573 S. Lake Ave., Pasadena, Calif. 91101. Editor: David Cutler. Issued monthly for retail lumber and building material dealers. Enclose S.A.S.E.
**Nonfiction:** Interested in articles and features of direct interest to specified audience; light, easy style; 1,000-1,500 words. Payment to be negotiated.

**WILSON LIBRARY BULLETIN,** 950 University Ave., Bronx, N.Y. 10452. Editor: William R. Eshelman. Issued monthly,

September through June; 75¢ per copy. 50% freelance. Copyrighted. Circulation: 39,000. Will send a free sample copy to a writer upon request. For professional librarians and those interested in the book and library worlds. Reports in two to eight weeks. Buys North American serial rights only. Pays on publication. Enclose S.A.S.E. for ms return. Ms must be original copy, double spaced; additional Xerox copy or carbon is appreciated. Special issues include Children's Literature issue, International Librarianship issue and Books in the Field (bibliographic essays) issues. Deadlines are a minimum of two months before publication.

**Nonfiction:** Uses articles of about 3,000-6,000 words of interest to librarians throughout the nation and around the world. Style must be lively, readable and sophisticated, with appeal to modern, socially-concerned professionals; facts must be thoroughly researched. Subjects range from the political to the comic in the world of media and libraries, with an emphasis on the human as well as the technical aspects of any story. No condescension: no library stereotypes. Pays about $50-$150 depending on the substance of article and its importance to readers. See "Books in the Field: Nature and Conservation," Oct. '69.

**Fiction:** Will consider short fiction with a strong library theme, but has yet to see any that avoids the usual library stereotypes. Payment as for articles.

**Poetry:** Will consider library verse or short poetry of the highest quality. Payment negotiated.

# Book Publishers

**°ACE BOOKS,** 1120 Avenue of the Americas, New York, N.Y. 10036. Vice-President in charge of Editorial: Donald A. Wollheim. A steady market for certain types of category fiction. (1) Science Fiction. As the largest publishers of this type of fiction in the field, Ace is looking for all types of novel from the light adventure interplanetary, the story of future civilizations and problems thereof, and off-trail themes having some element of scientific credibility. Uses a certain amount of good fantasy adventure a la Tolkien or Edgar Rice Burroughs also. "Sense of wonder is highly desirable, and we are also making a special push for quality of writing. Our rates are variable here, ranging from $1,250 for novels usable in our double books, to $1,500 for standard singles, and on up to a good deal more for very fine work capable of being packaged as Science Fiction Special." (2) Westerns—action-slanted stories of men against villainous opposition, stories of the rangeland West, with a feel for authenticity and a sense of the wide-open spaces. No sex-slant, Indian-fighting tales, cavalry yarns, nor tales north or south of the border. Period 1865-1900 only. About 45,000 words. (3) Nurse-romances—for a strictly female audience about girls in the nursing or medical profession finding true love. No sex scenes or suggestiveness. About 50,000 words. (4) Gothic romantic suspense novels—a field in which Ace was the originator. These are romantic novels of a damsel in distress somewhat akin to the Du Maurier romances. Quality counts here. (5) Mature romance novels for the Star line. (6) "Stranger Than Science" type of nonfiction books, dealing with phenomena, of such an unusual nature that science does not yet classify—flying saucers, Fortean news events, etc. Should be authentic and cite scources. Address science-fiction, Westerns, and nurse romances to Donald A. Wollheim, Editor. Gothic novels, mature

° Refers to publishers which also publish paperbacks.

romances, and "Stranger Than Science" books to Mrs. Evelyn Grippo, Editor of Ace Star Books. All advances are against regular royalty contracts. General advances range from $1,250 to $2,500. Reports within six weeks. Will consider sample chapters and detailed outlines, except for Ace Star submissions. Books published last year: 210.

°ATHENEUM PUBLISHERS, 122 E. 42nd St., New York, N.Y. 10017. All freelance submissions, with the exception of juveniles, should be addressed to the Editors. No word-length requirements, except that submission should be of book length. 40,000 words and over. For unsolicited mss prefer query, outline, or sample chapter. Reports on freelance submissions within four weeks. Publishes adult fiction, history, biography, science (for the layman), philosophy, the arts and general nonfiction. Juveniles should be submitted to Miss Jean Karl, Editor. Children's Books. No word length requirements and mss are accepted for all age levels. Special emphasis on the 8 to 12 readers. No interest in series books. Prefers finished books. Books published last year: 146.

°BANTAM BOOKS, INC., 666 Fifth Ave., New York, N.Y. 10019. Vice President and Editorial Director: Marc H. Jaffe; Assoc. Editorial Director: Allan Barnard. Executive Editor: Grace Bechtold. Publishes adult fiction and general nonfiction. No longer accepts unsolicited mss. Principally reprint. "Will consider, in special cases, mss, both fiction and nonfiction, which are aimed specifically at our market." Length: 75,000-100,000 words. Current catalogue available on request. Always send query giving details of the project. Reports in one month. Royalty 4% for first 150,000 copies sold; 6% thereafter. Books published last year: 280.

°BETTER HOMES AND GARDENS BOOKS, 1716 Locust St., Des Moines, Iowa 50303. Publishes hardcover and paperback originals. Nonfiction in all family and home service categories including money management, gardening, home building and improvement, decorating and remodeling, furnishings, sewing and crafts, health, travel, recreation and entertainment, pets, games, family legal matters, cooking and nutrition, and

other subjects of home service value. No specific length require-
ments. Send either outline and sample chapter or complete ms.
Address mss to Donald J. Dooley, Editorial Director. Reports
in three weeks. Royalty schedule varies with type of book prod-
uct. See representative titles: "BH&G Medical Guide," "BH&G
Photography Book," "BH&G Cook Book," "BH&G Sewing
Book," "BH&G Handyman's Book," "BH&G Baby Book," "BH
&G Story Book for Children," "BH&G Money Management
Book," "BH&G Decorating Book." Current catalogue available
on request.

°THE BOBBS-MERRILL CO., INC., 3 W. 57th St., New York,
N.Y. 10019. Editor-in-Chief: Robert Amussen. Hardcover and
paperback originals. Publishes American and foreign novels,
suspense, popular science, art criticism, theatre, film; religion,
both Catholic and Protestant; politics, history, and current
events, biography/autobiography. Children's Books Editor:
Miss Miriam Chaikin. Prefers complete mss if possible; otherwise query and outline on ideas. For preparation of ms, follow
instructions as listed in Chicago Style Manual. Reports on
mss within six weeks. Current leading titles include "The Glass
Virgin" by Cookson, "The Jocks" by Shecter, "The New Left"
by Teodori and "Madame De Maintenon" by Haldane. Will send
a catalogue on request. Books published last year: 50 adult, 22
juvenile.

BOUREGY, THOMAS, AND CO., INC., 22 E. 60th St., New
York, N.Y. 10022. Editor: Miss Reva Kindser. Publishes hard-
back orignals for teenagers and young adults. Publishes fiction:
romances, nurse and career stories, westerns and gothic novels.
Sensationalist elements should be avoided. Length: 50,000-
55,000 words. Query first. Also publishes Airmont Classics Series. $300 advance on publication date; 10% of retail price on all
copies after the original printing of 3,000, to which the $300
applies. Reports within one month. Books published last year:
50.

BRADBURY PRESS, INC., Englewood Cliffs, N.J. 07632. Vice
President and Editor-in-Chief: Richard W. Jackson. Hardcover
childrens books. "Fiction for children 2-12 is our major interest.

We publish little nonfiction, but will consider biographies, and science books for children 6-8. Picturebook texts may be only 1 to 2 typewritten pages. Novels can, of course, run 40,000 to 50,000 words." Reports within 16 weeks. Royalty payment. Current titles: "Portrait of Ivan," "Colors," "The Buried Moon."

\*CITADEL PRESS, 222 Park Ave. S., New York, N.Y. 10003. Publishes originals and reprints in both hardcover and paperbacks. In adult fiction, looks for characters of depth and color in finely-plotted, well-paced works that engross and that expose the accepted and unrecognized in daily life. Minimum of 60,000 words. In biographies, subject must be a figure of universal significance, and whether living or deceased, perspective must be the keynote in the recording of the life. 60,000 word minimum. Philosophical: only those thoughts and words which have the depth of meaning that makes them applicable to almost any peoples at any time. Word length varies according to subject and theme. Arts, techniques and developments within either the visual or the performing arts. Word length varies. Religion, only works offering information about the little-known religions of the world, or which attempt to bridge the gap between contemporary societies and the ancient beliefs. Minimum of 60,000 words. Always send a query with outline and sample chapter, and a S.A.S.E. Address all queries to Allan J. Wilson. Representative titles are "Bertold Brecht: His Life, His Art, and His Times," by Frederic Ewen, and "Mental Health through Nutrition," by Judge Tom R. Blaine. Reports on mss within 6 to 10 weeks. Royalty schedule: 10% of list price on first 7,500 copies sold; 12½% of list on copies sold between 7,501 and 12,000, and 15% on copies sold above 12,000. Books published last year: 52.

COWARD-McCANN, GEOGHEGAN, 200 Madison Ave., New York, N.Y. 10016. Editor-in-Chief: John J. Geoghegan. Publishes good full-length novels, including mysteries (no westerns or light or salacious love stories); outstanding nonfiction of all kinds; juveniles, but no novelty, toy, fantasy or stunt books; also publishes religious, history, biography (particularly on American figures). Also interested in humor. All should have general appeal. About 60,000 words, up. Pays on a royalty basis.

Send adult fiction, history and biography to John J. Geoghegan; juvenile mss to Miss Margaret Frith. Books published last year: 100.

**CROWN PUBLISHERS,** 419 Park Ave., S., New York, N.Y. 10016. Editor-in-Chief: Herbert Michelman; Senior Editors: Millen Brand, David McDowell, Nick Lyons; Special Projects: Brandt Aymar; Children's Books: Morrell Gipson. General fiction and nonfiction; pictorial histories, popular biography, science, and children's books. Also books on decorative arts and antiques, some on music, drama and painting. At least 50,000 words for adult material, 5,000-50,000 for juveniles. Prefers queries. Contracts offered on basis of stature of writer, outline, subject and sample material. Reports in 2 to 6 weeks. Address mss to department editor. Recent titles: "Savage Sleep" by Millen Brand, "A Pictorial History of The Theatre Guild" by Norman Nadel and "From Molecule To Man" by J.Z. Young and Tom Margerison. Will send catalogue on request. Books published last year: 125.

**DAY, JOHN, CO., INC.,** 257 Park Ave. S., New York, N.Y. 10010. Editor: Alan Tucker. Publishes juveniles, history, biography, science, general nonfiction and fiction (adult and young adult). Publishes hardcover originals only. Send outline and one or two sample chapters. Address mss to Editor. Reports within three weeks. Royalty schedule varies. Current catalogue available on request. Books published last year: 60.

**\*DELL PUBLISHING CO., INC.,** 750 Third Ave., New York, N.Y. 10017. Editorial Director: Ross Claiborne. Publishes adult fiction; general nonfiction including philosophy, biography, history, religion, science, the arts; juvenile. Publishes originals and reprints. Address mss to Ross Claiborne. Reports as soon as possible. Normal royalty schedule. Delacorte Press children's books: poetry, history, sports and science for ages 12 and over; history, social science and fiction for intermediate level; picture books for the very young. Length: 30,000-50,000 words for ages 12 to 16. George M. Nicholson, Juvenile Editor of Delacorte Press, wants completed mss for both nonfiction and fiction. Books published last year: 360.

°DOUBLEDAY AND CO., INC., 277 Park Ave., New York, N.Y. 10017. Editor-in-Chief: Ken McCormick. Interested in adult fiction, juvenile, history, biography, science, philosophy, religion, general nonfiction, cookbooks, westerns, science fiction and mysteries for the Crime Club series. Lengths vary for juveniles; for adult material, usually 75,000 words and up. All material goes to the Editorial Department, except for science (to the Science Editor), Catholic religious (to John Delaney, Catholic Image Books), Protestant and Jewish (to Alexander Liepa), cookbooks (to the Cookbook department) and juveniles (to the Books for Young Readers department). In the Dolphin line, have published a few original "handbooks" such as the "ABC's of Small Boat Sailing." "Career Guide for Young People" and "The Chicken Cook Book" and they are open for submissions in this area. Query first with letter, outline, sample chapters on nonfiction; complete ms on fiction. Also publishes °Anchor Books, quality paperback reprints. Pyke Johnson, Jr., Editor-in-Chief. Publishing division in collaboration with the American Museum of Natural History: °Natural History Press, publishes series dealing with all aspects of natural history, for juveniles and adults. Pays on a royalty basis. Usually reports within one month. Books published last year: 720.

°DUTTON, E.P., AND CO., INC., 201 Park Ave. S., New York, N.Y. 10003. Editor-in-Chief, adult publications: Hal Scharlatt; Juvenile Department: Ann Durrell. °Dutton Paperback: Cyril Nelson; other categories handled by John Macrae III. Publishes novels of permanent literary value; mystery, nonfiction, religious, travel, fine arts, biography, memoirs, belles lettres, history, science, psychology, translations, juveniles and quality paperbacks. Queries welcomed for nonfiction of high quality on almost any subject for the general reader. Before sending mss query with outline and sample chapters. Pays by advances and royalties. Current leading titles: "Pricksongs and Descants" by Robert Coover, "Robert Kennedy: A Memoir" by Jack Newfield and "The Book of Imaginary Beings" by Jorge Luis Borges.

°FAWCETT PUBLICATIONS, INC., 67 W. 44th St., New York, N.Y. 10036. Editor, Gold Medal Books: Walter Fultz. Wants taut, intriguing novels of mystery and suspense with a solid, professional polish to the writing, compelling characters, and an imaginative, freshly conceived plot. Also, straight novels with real dramatic "pull", convincing people and exciting situations. Also publishes westerns with strong conflicts, and which demonstrate a real feeling for the old West. Wants science-fiction material—novels as well as collections and anthologies of stories. 60,000-70,000 words. Also wants nonfiction books of general topical interest for mass-market distribution—photography, biography, cartoon books, puzzle and game books, novelty items, humor, etc. Send outlines and sample chapters to Gold Medal Books. Crest is Fawcett's reprint line, though Gold Medal does occasionally publish reprints. Pays $2,500 advance against royalties of 4% of the book's retail price for the first 200,000 copies printed (not sold) and 6% of the retail price thereafter. Reports within one month.

*GROSSET AND DUNLAP, INC.,* 51 Madison Ave., New York, N.Y. 10010. Editor-in-Chief: Lewis Gillenson; Managing Editor: Joseph Greene; Editors, trade dept.: David Goodnough, Kevin Curley, Jacques Bartlett, Donald Davidson, Alice Thorne, Anne Hagan, Thetis Powers; Assistant Editors: Wendy May, Claire Bazinet, Barbara Zahler; Editor-in-Chief, Children's Picture Books: Doris Duenewald; Editor, *Tempo Paperbacks: Charlotte Gordon. Publishes general nonfiction including history, science, religion, biography, the arts, literature, sports and reprints. Also publishes reprints and original "Specials" in paperback (on useful current subjects): *Tempo Teenage paperbacks and *Universal Library (quality paperbacks). Send outline with sample chapters. Address to Lewis Gillenson. Reports in three to five weeks. Royalty and advance varies. Current catalogue available. Books published last year: 308.

*HARPER AND ROW PUBLISHERS, INC.,* 49 E. 33rd St., New York, N.Y. 10016. Publishes books between 40,000 and 200,000 words in the following departments: Children's Books, College, Elementary and High School, Mail Order, Medical, Nature & Outdoor, Religious, Social & Economic, and Trade. Trade books can cover any subject of general interest, fiction or nonfiction. Royalty schedule subject to negotiation, but generally 10% to 5,000; 12½% to 10,000; 15% thereafter. Reports in four to six weeks. Query letters, sample chapters and outlines preferred. Harper and Row also publishes *Torchbooks, *Colophon and *Perennial Library (paperback lines). Ursula Nordstrom, Juvenile Editor. El-Hi Division, 2500 Crawford Ave., Evanston, Ill. Landon Risteen, Publisher; publishes elementary and high school textbooks. Trade books should be of general interest, rather than specialized or scholarly works. Address General Trade Dept. for fiction and nonfiction. For fiction, send completed ms. Include S.A.S.E. for return. For juveniles, address to the Children's Book Dept. Publishes paperback reprints.

*HAWTHORN BOOKS, INC., 70 Fifth Ave., New York, N.Y. 10011. Vice President and Editorial Director: Paul Fargis. Publishes general nonfiction in the fields of antiques, biography, history, cooking, gardening, reference, science, self-help, and religious books for trade and mail order. Length: 50,000 words and up. Also publishes juveniles; send to Children's Book Editor. Send query accompanied by outline and sample chapter. Strongly suggests consulting catalogue before making any submission. Has new line of quality paperbacks, consisting of reprints from back list; may later include original paperbacks as well. Reports in one month. Normal advance and royalty schedule. Current catalogue available. Books published last year: 89.

*LANCER BOOKS, INC., 1560 Broadway, New York, N.Y. 10036. Editors: Evan Heyman and Robert Hoskins. Completed mss from writers of established reputations only; otherwise, full query. Publishes reprints, originals, adult fiction, biographies of topical personalities (on assignment only). Likes fiction in all standard categories and an occasional completely offbeat novel. Standard 4% and 6% royalty schedule. Reports in 2-6 weeks. Books published last year: 250.

*MACFADDEN-BARTELL CORP., 205 East 42nd St., New York, N.Y. 10017. Editor-in-Chief: George A. Glay. Publishes paperback reprints and originals, both fiction and nonfiction. Please query before sending mss. Books published last year: 154.

**°McGRAW-HILL BOOK COMPANY,** 330 West 42nd St., New York, N.Y. 10036. Publishes fiction, history, biography, belles lettres, general nonfiction, how-to, travel, popular references, inspirational, art, and religious books. Representative titles: "Soul on Ice," Cleaver; "The Joys of Yiddish," Rosten, "Ada," Nabokov; "Obsolete Communism," Cohn-Bendit; "The Interior Landscape," McLuhan; "The Human Zoo," Monia; "The Link," Maughm; "Fake," Irving. Also publishes McGraw-Hill Junior Books.

**°NEW AMERICAN LIBRARY,** 1301 Avenue of the Americas, New York, N.Y. 10019. President: Sidney B. Kramer. Publishes paperback original and reprint adult fiction and general nonfiction. Send paperback submission queries to Edward T. Chase, Editorial Vice President. Signet Books: Modern novels and topical nonfiction. Signet Classics: World masterpieces of fiction. Mentor Books: Distinquished nonfiction by outstanding authorities, in such fields as archaeology, anthropology, psychology, economics, religion, philosophy, history, science, and the arts. Mentor Classics: New translations of Greek, Roman, and other ancient enduring works. Originals generally commissioned; best to query before submitting. Send query or outline for nonfiction; query for fiction. Reports in about two weeks. Pays standard paperback royalties. Leading current titles: "True Grit," "The Confessions of Nat Turner," "The Armies of the Night." Current catalogue available on request. Books published last year: 365.

**°POCKET BOOKS,** 630 Fifth Ave., New York, N.Y. 10020. Paperback originals and reprints on history, biography, philosophy, general nonfiction and adult fiction. Some biography, reference books, joke books, mysteries. Current titles: "The Raw Pearl," Pearl Bailey; "The Horse Is Dead," Robert Klane; "By the Pricking of My Thumbs," Agatha Christie; "The Husband," Sol Stein. Reports in one to three months. Books published last year: 175.

**°RANDOM HOUSE, INC.,** 201 East 50th St., New York, N.Y. 10022. Chairman of the Board: Bennett Cerf; Vice-Chairman: Donald Klopfer; President: Robert Bernstein; Vice President and Editorial Director: Albert Erskine; Vice President and Editor-in-Chief: James H. Silberman; Vice President and Managing Editor: C.A. Wimpfheimer; Senior Editors: Jason Epstein, Robert Loomis, Joseph Fox, John Simon, Lee Wright, Charles Harris, Nan Talese, Charlotte Meyerson. Publishes fiction and nonfiction of the highest standards. Not interested in circulating library material. Publishes occasional poetry volumes. Payment as per contracts. Publishes a paperback line, °Vintage Books. Jason Epstein, John Simon, Editors. Paperback reprints and originals. Send complete ms. Publishes a broad range of fiction and nonfiction for young readers, including Beginner Books, Step-up Books, Gateway Books, Landmark Books. Particularly interested in high-quality fiction for children. Walter Retan, Executive Editor; Janet Finnie, Senior Editor.

°SCHOLASTIC BOOK SERVICES, 50 West 44th St., New York, N.Y. 10036. Growing markets are: Four Winds Press, See-Saw Book Club, Teen Age Book Club, Lucky Club, Campus Book Club, Arrow Book Club and Citation Press. Scholastic is seeking more and more original material. Editorial requirements: fiction and nonfiction ranging from pre-school picture book level to adult. Subjects for juvenile and young adult books should be limited to those acceptable to these audiences. A minimum of 32 pages for a picture book with a few words on each page to a maximum of 100,000 words or more for a full-length adult book. Books for young adult readers should be limited to 60,000 words. Middle grade books should be about 30,000 words. Scope/Action books needs fiction of 8,000-12,000 words written for secondary school students who read at second to fourth grade level. No writing down. Settings and characters with which average teens can identify. Emphasis on action, as the series' title suggests. See-Saw Book Club for grades kindergarten and first needs science picture books. Lucky Book Club for grades second and third interested in science, mystery, adventure. Arrow Book Club for fourth, fifth and sixth grade readers wants science, biography and mystery. The elementary clubs also looking for authors interested in writing books on Negro history on Negro contributions in general. Also fiction with an honest minority group point of view or with legitimate minority group characters. Teen Age Book Club for grades 7-9 needs humor (fiction and nonfiction) and nonfiction on pop music, cars, hot-rodding, movie and TV personalities, beauty tips, teen grooming, pro sports. Fiction needed about adolescent concerns of school, friends, family, dating; also mystery and suspense novels. Campus Book Club for grades 10-12 needs humor, superior romances for older girls, nonfiction about the contemporary scene, suspense novels, fiction and nonfiction about adolescent problems, action-filled nonfiction for boys about man's efforts to survive. All these should be written on fairly adult level. Editorial requirements for science mss: nonfiction, curriculum oriented, on the juvenile or young adult level, suitable for supplementary reading or use in class as project material. Mss should deal with research and involve the work of scientists today. Style should be lively, colorful, informative; not textbookish. Citation Press focuses on trends, innovations and new programs at all levels of education for teachers, administrators and college students in teacher education. Scholastic's standard contract for paperback rights provides for an advance against royalties which ranges, depending on the book's market potential, upward from $500. Paperback royalties start at 4% of the selling price. Scholastic's contracts are often made for both hard and softcover publications. Hardcover royalties begin at 10%. Please address mss and inquiries to Mrs. Norma R. Ainsworth, Editor of Manuscript Department.

**SHERBOURNE PRESS, INC.,** 1640 S. La Cienega Blvd., Los Angeles, Calif. 90035. Publishes hardcover originals only. Adult fiction must have well-defined characters and conflicts. Not interested in westerns, spy novels. Seeks juvenile novels for an audience of at least 14 years and up. Length: 60,000-100,000 words. Also quality science fiction, but no plots to destroy the world by monsters, and no stories of alien cultures in which more is told of the alien culture than of the story. Science fiction length: 50,000-85,000 words. History, same length as fiction. Biography, 60,000 to 100,000 words; "not the nicest lady on the block or 'my favorite uncle'." Science, if suited to lay audience and about topical subjects. Not interested in flouridation-as-a-Communist-plot kind of science. Length can go as high as 85,000 words. Philosophy must be rationally motivated, topical, with sense of regard for human dignity. 60,000 to 85,000 words. The arts, 50,000 to 100,000 words. General nonfiction, 60,000 to 100,000 words. Exposé, how-to, self-help. "For the Millions" series consists of primer-introductory texts on the occult and ESP subjects; 60,000 words. Mss for this series only are purchased on an outright sale basis. Standard royalties for others: 10% to 12½%, 15%. For nonfiction send outline and sample chapter. Send completed mss for fiction to Mr. Shelly Lowenkopf. See suggestions in "Words into Type" by Skillin, Gay, et al, Appleton-Century-Crofts, or the University of Chicago "Manual of Style." Use only one type face for each ms, clean white ms paper, good ribbon. Must include S.A.S.E. for ms return. Will not read handwritten letters or mss. Reports in 8-10 weeks. Current titles to watch as indications of preferences: Dr. Grant Gwinup's "Energetics: Your Key to Weight Control," W. Turner's "Hoover's F.B.I.: The Men and the Myth," Steve Fisher's "Saxon's Ghost" and "A Wilderness of Stars." Happy to send catalog on request. Books published last year: 27.

# Greeting Card Publishers

**AMERICAN GREETINGS CORPORATION,** 1300 W. 78th St., Cleveland, Ohio 44102. Editorial Director: Carl Goeller. Pays top rates for humorous ideas and cute or humorous greeting-book material. No conventional verse. Send studio ideas to Tom Wilson, Hi-Brow editor. Must be of professional quality. Not a large freelance market, mostly staff-written material, but does purchase a limited number of highly original studio ideas. "We do like to keep the door open for interesting, unusual material." Pays upon acceptance. Prompt replies. Also in the market for strong ideas for $1 greeting books called Little Sunbeam books. Generally have a "from-me-to-you" message, i.e., missing you, love you, happy birthday, etc. Many of a friendship nature, paying a compliment to a friend or offering inspiration. Special books for holiday greetings. Copy should be simple and charming. Suggests study books available in department stores, etc. Rates vary with the idea, but normally run between $50-$100 per book. No royalty arrangements made for these books. Enclose S.A.S.E.

**BARKER GREETING CARD CO.,** 31st and Robertson Ave., Cincinnati, Ohio 45209. Editor: George Wilson. Publishes cards for everyday and all seasons. Wants fresh and original ideas for studio line. Some risqués, but only if funny. Not interested in art work. Pays $20 up on acceptance, extra for ideas with mechanical or new attachments. Reports in two weeks. Buys all rights. Enclose S.A.S.E.

**CHARM CRAFT PUBLISHERS, INC.,** 33 35th St., Brooklyn, N.Y. 11232. Humor and Studio Editor: Mrs. Marilyn Freda. Publishes all types of cards. Enclose S.A.S.E. Pays $1 a line for conventional verse, top prices for humorous and studio ideas. Returns rejects within 10 days, but holds may take up to 60 days.

**GIBSON GREETING CARDS, INC.,** 2100 Section Road, Cincinnati, Ohio 45237. Address Editor. Interested in outstanding studio, humorous, and general material. Prices increase when accompanied with unusual design and/or mechanical ideas such as trick folds, die cuts, shapes, or attachments and little or no reworking is required. Straight verse $1.50 per line and up, depending on originality, suitability for publication and required amount of editing. Payment on acceptance. Reports within 10 days. Buys exclusive rights. Pays $20 for humorous verse alone, $25 for verse plus sketch. $30 for mechanic, $25 for studio. Enclose S.A.S.E.

**HALLMARK CARDS, INC.,** Contemporary Department, 25th & McGee, Kansas City, Mo. 64141. Managing Editor: Kent De-Vore. Pays $50 for crisp, sendable, contemporary ideas fitting all everyday and seasonal needs. Looking for unusual, sophisticated, humorous material. Avoid slam, ethnic, sarcastic, and off-color ideas. Enclose S.A.S.E.

**THE PARAMOUNT LINE, INC.,** Box 678, Pawtucket, R.I. 02862. Editor: Mrs. Dorothy M. Nelson. Interested in everyday material at all times. Seasonal verses read on approximately the following schedule: Easter, Mother's Day, Father's Day, and Graduation during September through February; Thanksgiving, Christmas, and New Year during February through June; Valentine's Day and St. Patrick's Day during July through September. Verses should not exceed 8 lines in length. Rate of payment starts at $1 a line. For humorous and studio ideas, ability to present your ideas in the form of a rough sketch substantially increases the rate of payment. Buys all rights. Reports within two weeks. Enclose S.A.S.E. Instruction sheet available for freelance contributors; include S.A.S.E. with your request.

**REED STARLINE CARD CO.,** 3331 Sunset Blvd., Los Angeles, Calif. 90026. Needs original studio card copy that is short, conversational in tone, and written for sophisticated adults—including the 20-25 year olds—either smart and humorous, or cute and sweet. Submit each idea on 3x5 card. Copy must carry a message. Original studio card art work may also be submitted. Payment for art work is $80 for each piece of copy, art and color separation; $40 for color separation only, on acceptance. Submit designs to finished size: 3¾ x 8⅝". Screen tints, halftones, etc. are acceptable. Categories include birthday, friendship, get well, anniversary, thank you, travel and congratulations, plus all seasons. Pays $40 per idea on acceptance. Monthly cash prizes for top-selling "everyday" copy. Seasonal prizes for copy $100, $50 and $25. Information sheet available for writers and artists. Include stamped, self-addressed return envelope with all submissions and requests.

**RUST CRAFT GREETING CARDS, INC.,** Rust Craft Road, Dedham, Mass. 02026. Editor: Dolores Anderson. Top rates for humorous, studio, general, religious and juvenile cards. Publishes monthly market letter in each area; free upon receipt of stamped, self-addressed envelope. Include name and address and numerical code on each individual contribution. Enclose stamped, self-addressed envelope for ms return. $1.25 per line for general verse, $10 for informal cards, $30 for humorous verses, $25 for studio ideas. Buys all rights. Pays on acceptance. Reports promptly. Enclose S.A.S.E.

**VAGABOND CREATIONS,** 2560 Lance Drive, Dayton, Ohio 45409. Editor: George F. Stanley, Jr. Publishes contemporary cards. Studio verse only; no slams, puns, or reference to age or aging. Emphasis should be placed on a strong surprise inside punch line instead of one that is predictable. Also prefers good use of double entendre. Rate of payment for verse begins at $10; same for art, $20 for art and verse, if both used. Purchases copy for everydays, Christmas, Valentine's and Graduation. Also very interested in receiving copy for mottoes, note pads, humorous buttons. Same rate of pay as for cards. Purchases all rights. Reports the same week as received. Copy should be written in the "first person" about situations at the job, about the job, confusion, modest bragging, and drinking habits, among others. Enclose S.A.S.E.

# Cartoonists Wanting Gags

**ARENTS, BOB,** 4141 Thomas St., Hollywood, Fla. 33021. A good minor-market man who has graduated to the middle markets. "I can use general stuff—but it must be good enough for at least the $25 markets before I'll draw it up. I pay 25%." Enclose S.A.S.E.

**BACAL, AARON,** 305 Ocean Parkway, Brooklyn, N.Y. 11218. Interested in seeing large batches of gags. Please, no tired and trite situations—for generals, wants clever, topical gags. For trade journals, wants a minimum of 5-6 with same slant. Reports in one week. Pays 30% commission. Enclose S.A.S.E.

**BAGINSKI, FRANK,** Box 108, Village Station, New York, N.Y. 10014. Uses all types of gags. Will look at typewritten gag slips in batches of twelve. Pays 25%. Also will buy gags (old, unsold, beaten up) for a flat $1 a piece. Major markets include True, Cavalier, True Detective, King and Signature. Sometimes holds checks until they accumulate. Enclose S.A.S.E.

**BOND, DOROTHY, ENTERPRISES,** 2450 N. Washtenaw Ave., Chicago, Ill. 60647. Always interested in high-humor, good gags with unusual twist. "Nothing sexy, please, for we sell to top-grade women's magazines. Return postage must accompany submissions. We pay 60% to us and 40% to you. Your submission reviewed, accepted or returned immediately. Career girls and housewives also invited to send funny happenings in their day . . . these make into excellent magazine cartoon sales. Male gag writers equally welcome."

**BRUMMER, FRANCIS H. (RUM),** Box 191, Missouri Valley, Iowa 51555. Would like to see batches of not over 30 gags. "Try all types of trade gags, insurance, food processing, chemicals, manufacturing, farm, auto, engineering, construction, teen-age, religious, Sunday school, etc. Also auto safety, farm safety, plant safety and child safety. Pays 30% to top five writers per previous year sales; 25% to others. Also 50-50 plan. Gag writer sells the gag and I draw up and send to editor for 50%." Enclose S.A.S.E.

**GORDON, MAL,** 29 Monroe Ave., Worcester, Mass. 01602. Will look at batches of 10 gags, no sexy or girly gags. Looking for gags for minor, major and middle markets: has sold Rotarian, Journal of the American Dental Association, Home Garden, NEA Journal, Datamation, Today's Health, Case and Comment, etc. Would like to see gags on: Computer type gags; sophisticated educational—college and grade school level; medical and dental; pertaining to lawyers and the legal profession; garden type humor; general everyday humor; pays 25%. Enclose S.A.S.E.

**KATZMAN, LARRY "KAZ",** 101 Central Park West, Apt. 4B, New York, N.Y. 10023. Has been selling cartoons for 20 years. Uses gagwriters extensively and encourages submissions. Any amount per batch. Mr. Katzman wants only medical, nurse, hospital, drug store, and drug gags. Mild sex is okay in a medical category. He uses hundreds of these type gags per year for his regular Nellie Nifty, R.N., feature and other medical and drug features. He pays standard 25% commission plus bonus when gags are re-used in his Dell paperback collections. Enclose S.A.S.E.

**MORIN, RAY,** 140 Hamilton Ave., Meriden, Conn. 06450. His major markets include Good Housekeeping, Boys' Life, Parade, etc. Will look at batches of 8-10 gags; domestics, kids, teenagers, adventure, family. No girlie or sex gags. All good taste material. 25% commission. Stamped, self-addressed envelope must accompany material.

**TOWNSEND, MARVIN,** 631 West 88th St., Kansas City, Mo. 64114. Sells mostly to business and trade magazines of all types, and has done this for the past 25 years. Would like to see batches of a dozen gags each, with a trade journal or business slant, caption or captionless. Don't waste postage sending worn out gags or non-professional material. Will sell and pay 25% for good gags. Enclose S.A.S.E.

**WINBURG, ART,** 21 McKinley Ave., Jamestown, N.Y. 14701. Will look at all types of gags; general, house organs, trade journals, children's magazines. Batches of 15-18. No raw sex gags. 25-30% commission. Twenty-five years of experience selling to Redbook, American Legion Magazine, Successful Farming, Farm Journal, VFW, Boys' Life, Sport and Better Homes and Gardens, trade journals and house organs. Enclose S.A.S.E.

# Play Publishers

**CHELSEA**, P. O. Box 242, Old Chelsea Sta., New York, N.Y. 10011. Address Editor. Publishes short plays—or in excerpt—not exceeding 20 pages. Must possess quality, according to editor's taste. Pays in copies. Reports in about one month. Enclose S.A.S.E.

**CONTEMPORARY DRAMA SERVICE, ARTHUR MERIWETHER, INC.,** Box 457, Downers Grove, Ill. 60515. Editor: Arthur L. Zapel, Jr. Interested in one-act plays or drama presentations for all age levels on subjects of religion, current affairs and/or social dilemmas, suitable for staging with little or no scenery or costumes. Prefers experimental treatment and staging, original, off-beat approach and solid writing backed by mature thinking. Buys all rights. Pays 10% royalty up to first $250 and 5% royalty thereafter. Reporting time varies; sometimes within two days and never longer than one month, even during busy season. Enclose S.A.S.E.

**DENISON, T.S., COMPANY, INC.,** 5100 W. 82nd St., Minneapolis, Minn. 55431. Editor: L.M. Brings. Interested in unusual types of entertainment skits and stunts for amateur use. Children's stories coordinated with units of study in the classroom. Pays outright upon acceptance. Reports within one month. Enclose S.A.S.E.

**ELDRIDGE PUBLISHING COMPANY,** Franklin, Ohio 45005. Editor: Kay Myerly. Wants good three-act and one-act plays. Special day, church, and school entertainments for all ages and all occasions. Unusual plots, snappy dialogue, good curtains. Enclose S.A.S.E. for ms return. Cash payment on acceptance. Reports within 90 days when possible.

**FRENCH, SAMUEL,** 25 W. 45th St., New York, N.Y. 10036. Editors: William Talbot and Jack Walsh. Willing at all times to read manuscripts of books concerning the theater, as well as manuscripts of plays. No reading fee. All manuscripts must be typewritten (in English) on one side of the sheet only. All manuscripts are read, as a rule, within 6-8 weeks of receipt. In addition to publishing plays, also acts as agents in the placement of plays for Broadway production, and of program series for television production. Enclose S.A.S.E.

**THE HEUER PUBLISHING COMPANY,** Drawer 248, Cedar Rapids, Iowa 52406. Editor: Edward I. Heuer. Wants 1-act and 3-act farce comedy, and mystery plays suitable for high school production. One simple set. Authors should write for free leaflet, "Type of Plays Required for the Amateur Stage." Prompt reports. Cash payment on acceptance, from $100 for 1-act play to $1,000 for first-class 3-act play. Enclose S.A.S.E.

**INSTRUCTOR PUBLICATIONS, INC.,** (The INSTRUCTOR Magazine), Dansville, N.Y. 11437. Editor: R. Pratt Krull, Jr. Will consider any type play suitable for presentation in elementary schools by children from 4 to 14. Most are from 10 to 25 minutes playing time, but occasionally interested in longer productions. Limited music—melody of one or two songs. Interested especially in dramatic material that offers opportunities for creativity—ideas for play frameworks on which children can build. Subject matter should reflect the serious nature of education today, and the current interests of children. Fairies and fantasy are temporarily out of favor. Assembly program suggestions and seasonal plays welcomed. Freelance writers outside the educational field should consult qualified persons in regard to educational value of script before submitting. Payments range from $20 to $50. Buys all publication rights. Reprinting in books is subject to company's approval. Keeps out of filmstrips, film, radio and TV sales. Tries to report in two weeks. Decisions to use may be reached in three months. Seasonal material is selected five or six months in advance of month used. Enclose S.A.S.E.

**McKAY, DAVID, CO., INC.,** 750 Third Ave., New York, N.Y.

10017. Well-written, clean, one-act and three-act plays. Preferably those which have been tried out successfully in local production and are suitable for all types of amateur groups. More women than men are desirable in the cast. Payment individually on the basis of each script. Reports in 4-6 weeks. Enclose S.A.S.E.

**PIONEER DRAMA SERVICE,** Cody, Wyo. 82414. Editor and Publisher: Shubert Fendrich. Needs one-act plays, mainly for high school market, with either an almost balanced cast or more women than men. Submissions limited to those plays that have had successful productions on either amateur or professional stage. Play scripts should be accompanied by production record, list of credits and reviews. Also plays about an hour in length for Children's Theatre, to be produced by adults or older children for younger children. Also uses old fashioned melodrama. Offers royalty on all copies sold, plus 50% of re-sale rights. (TV, softcover, etc.) Reports in 30-60 days. Include S.A. S.E. for return.

**PLAYS INC.:** The Drama Magazine for Young People, 8 Arlington Street, Boston, Mass. 02116. Publishes approximately 100 one-act plays each season. Interested in buying good plays for young people of all age groups—junior and senior high, middle grades, lower grades. In addition to comedies, farces, mysteries and dramas, can use plays for holidays and other special occasions. Adaptations of classic stories and fables, historical plays, plays about other lands, plays for an all-girl or all-boy cast, plays dramatizing factual information and on such themes as good citizenship, tolerance and patriotism are needed. Prefers one scene; when more than one is necessary, changes should be simple. Manuscripts should follow the general style of Plays Magazine. They should be typewritten, double-spaced with wide margins, one side of the page only. Stage directions should not be typed in capital letters or underlined. Every play ms should include: a list of characters, an indication of time, a description of setting; an "At Rise," describing what is taking place on stage as curtain rises; production notes, indicating the number of characters and the playing time, describing the costumes, properties, setting and special lighting effects, if any.

Playwrights should not use incorrect grammar or dialect. Characters with physical defects, speech impediments should not be included. Desired lengths for mss are: Junior and Senior high —20 to 25 double-spaced ms pages (25 to 30 minutes playing time). Middle Grades—12 to 15 pages (15 to 20 minutes playing time). Lower Grades—6 to 10 pages (8 to 15 minutes playing time). Pays good rates on acceptance. Query first. Reports in three to four weeks. Enclose S.A.S.E.

# Syndicates

**BELL-McCLURE SYNDICATE**, 1501 Broadway, New York, N.Y. 10036. Editor-in-Chief: Elmer Roessner. Buys on contract with authors and artists to supply features for newspapers. Reports within 21 days, often sooner. Pays 50% on a contract basis. Buys U.S. and Canadian rights, sometimes world rights. Enclose S.A.S.E.

**Nonfiction:** Wants long-term features, not short-term or single features. Currently syndicating Jack Anderson's "Washington Merry-Go-Round," Dr. Joyce Brothers, Harry Golden, and 50 other features.

**Fiction:** Does not use fiction except for rare condensation of a best seller.

**Fillers:** Puzzles.

**CHICAGO TRIBUNE-NEW YORK NEWS SYNDICATE, INC.,** 220 East 42nd St., New York, N.Y. 10017. Editor: Arthur Laro. Reports promptly. Enclose S.A.S.E.

**Nonfiction:** Looking for short, promotable news and feature series for newspapers, columns. Pays 50% of gross revenue. Rights negotiated.

**FEATURE NEWS SERVICE**, 2330 S. Brentwood Blvd., St. Louis, Mo. 63144. Editor: George G. White, Sr. Buys all rights. Reports promptly. Enclose S.A.S.E.

**Nonfiction:** Looking for articles of interest to strictly rural readers in midwest for weekly newspapers. Also looking for articles for trade association publications relating to foreign travel and coin car wash. Length: 300-500 words. "A single feature would be purchased only on a 'contingent' basis since we have heavier expenses in placing a single article in various rural newspapers. Payment would only be made based on contingency that feature is run and the revenue derived therefrom. Query first before sending material or articles. Payment subject to negotiation.

**GENERAL FEATURES CORPORATION,** Times Mirror Square,
Square, Los Angeles, Calif. 90053. Chief Editor: Ed Grade.
Syndicators of the Paul Harvey, Jenkin Lloyd Jones and Rus-
sell Kirk columns; Sydney Omarr astrology feature and Shein-
wold bridge. Buys newspaper syndication rights. Reports within
two weeks. Enclose S.A.S.E.
**Nonfiction:** Buys columns. Interested in fresh and original features of a continuing nature. Contract arrangements are made
in payment for material.

**KING FEATURES SYNDICATE,** 235 E. 45th St., New York,
N.Y. 10017. Enclose S.A.S.E.
**Nonfiction:** Submit new features to Neal Freeman, Executive
Editor.
**Photos:** Photographs purchased by Louis Messolonghites, As-
sistant to the Executive Editor.

**LOS ANGELES TIMES SYNDICATE,** Times Mirror Square,
Los Angeles, Calif. 90053. Chief Editor: Ed Grade. Syndicators
of the Art Buchwald, Joseph Alsop columns. Buys newspaper
syndication rights. Reports within two weeks. Enclose S.A.S.E.
**Nonfiction:** Buys columns. Interested in fresh and original features of a continuing nature. Contract arrangements are made
in payment for material.

**MEREDITH ASSOCIATES INC.,** P. O. Box 361, Rutherford,
N.J. 07070. Editorial Director: George Meredith. Seeking correspondents in all parts of the country (except New York, New
Jersey, Connecticut) to handle writing and reporting assignments ranging from simple telephone interviews to writing
case history features. Material needed for clients' dealer house
organs, association newsletters, marketing research studies,
magazine survey reports, etc. No speculation; intends to build
a list of qualified writers able to accept assignments on occasion. Payment negotiable, from $5 for brief reports to $100 for
complete features. Most of the projects are in the marketing,
merchandising, or sales promotion fields.
**NORTH AMERICAN NEWSPAPER ALLIANCE,** 1501 Broadway St., New York, N.Y. 10036. Editor: Sid Goldberg. Daily
file to leading U.S. and Canadian newspapers, also to South
America, Europe, Asia and Africa. Buys Newspaper syndication rights. Reports within two weeks. Enclose S.A.S.E.

**Nonfiction and Photos:** In the market for background, interpretive and news features. The news element must be strong and purchases are generally made only from experienced, working newspapermen. Wants timely news features of national interest that do not duplicate press association coverage but add to it, interpret it, etc. Wants first-class nonfiction suitable for feature development. The story must be aimed at newspapers, must be self-explanatory, factual and well condensed. It must add measurably to the public's information or understanding of the subject, or be genuinely entertaining. Broad general interest is the key to success here. Rarely buys columns. Looking for good one-shots and good series of two to seven articles. Where opinions are given, the author should advise, for publication, his qualifications to comment on specialized subjects. Article should keep within 800 words if possible, under 400 preferred. The news must be exclusive to be considered at all. Rate varies depending on length and news value. Minimum rate $25, but will go considerably higher for promotable copy. Buys 8x10 glossy photos when needed to illustrate story. Pays $5-$10 each.

**UNITED FEATURE SYNDICATE, INC.,** 220 E. 42nd St., New York, N.Y. 10017. Associate Editor: Charles D. Treleven. Buys world rights; first serial rights on assigned series, second serial rights on published books. Reports within ten days. Enclose S.A.S.E.
**Nonfiction:** Three-part to six-part series (1,000 words per article), on high-impact subjects of broad general interest. Human interest, how-to, personalities. Outlines first to Charles D. Treleven. Pays $300 per series.

**WORLD BOOK SCIENCE SERVICE,** 820 Chronicle Bldg., Houston, Texas 77002. Editor: William J. Cromie. Syndicates to 110 U.S. newspapers and numerous foreign publications. Pays on acceptance. Enclose S.A.S.E.
**Nonfiction:** Interested in seeing one-page queries from qualified and experienced writers. General stories, related to all aspects of science, including behavioral research and the roles of science in politics, government, economics and business. Pays from $50 to $300 for final copy of 300 to 2,500 words. More for outstanding and exclusive stories.
**Photos:** Pays extra for first class photographs to illustrate stories.

# Contributing Authors

### George Abraham

George Abraham's first job out of college was as editor of a horticulture trade journal. He then became a writer on garden subjects for the Sunday New York Times. During Army service he was a correspondent for *Yank* and then on discharge worked for an advertising agency before establishing his own "Green Thumb" syndicated column. With his wife, Katy, he has had a horticulture radio program for 25 years in Rochester and is also seen there on television.

### Arvel Ahlers

Arvel Ahlers jumped into free-lance writing (both fiction and nonfiction) straight from college for three years till the Navy tapped him for service. A former editor on the staff of FARM QUARTERLY, WRITER'S DIGEST and MICHIGAN MODERN PHOTOGRAPHY, he then joined J. Walter Thompson Advertising Agency as a copywriter, then account executive. He is now the executive editor of Famous Photographers Schools. He is the author of eight published books including *Where and How to Sell Your Pictures* and *How and Where to Sell Your Pictures Overseas*.

### James Boeringer

James Boeringer teaches at Susquehanna University in Selinsgrove, Pa. He has for the past nine years been Editorial Assistant in charge of reviews for the *American Guild of Organists' Quarterly*, with concurrent briefer stints as a free-lance critic for the *Musical Courier*, the *New York Times*, the *Daily Oklahoman*, and other papers and magazines.

### H. Joseph Chadwick

A former technical writer in the electronics industry, the author started freelancing studio greeting card ideas and eventually became so good at it he gave up technical writing to become editor of Barker Greeting Cards. He is now Director of Writer's Digest Schools, which offers correspondence courses in article and short story writing.

## Don Cullimore

The author began writing 35 years ago in the fields of both pulp fiction and trade journals while still a newspaperman. He has, today, over 500 magazine article credits and five books. He is executive director of the Outdoor Writers Association.

## Jean Davison

The author has been selling crosswords since 1952. Her puzzles appear in TV Guide and the Dell magazines. Currently she is at work on a book of specialty crosswords.

## Alan W. Eckert

Allan W. Eckert, of Englewood Beach, Florida, is the author of fourteen books on American history and natural history subjects. Four of his books—A TIME OF TERROR, WILD SEASON, THE FRONTIERSMEN, and WILDERNESS EMPIRE—have received Pulitzer Prize nominations and, though he has never won that coveted award, he has won others.

Three of Mr. Eckert's books are currently being made into movies for theater showing. These three are: THE FRONTIERSMEN (Warner Brothers Seven Arts); THE CROSS BREED (Don Meier Productions), and BLUE JACKET (Thomas Smith Productions).

Mr. Eckert has worked as a newspaper reporter, columnist and editor and in 1960 he entered the free-lance magazine writing field on a full-time basis. His articles and short stories have appeared in most of the major magazines in the United States, and in some foreign periodicals.

## Joan Potter Elwart

The author's own five children along with those she taught in elementary school provided an excellent background for her juvenile writing. Her stories have appeared in most of the popular children's magazines and her books have been published by Whitman and Steck-Vaughn.

## Mary Louise Foley

"Since 1958, I have been writing TV, radio, publicity and retail copy on assignment for the Sacramento market, plus freelancing light verse, greeting cards and 'domestic' articles . . . with inspiration supplied by two sons, one dog and one very talented husband (Public Information Officer for the City of Sacramento) who, thank goodness, shares my enthusiasm for writing."

## Paul H. Fugleberg

The author is a Montana freelance writer-photographer. Using the techniques described in his article, he has sold articles to the New York Times, Westways, Christian Science Monitor, Grit and numerous regional newspapers.

## Robert Hays

The author is head of the English Department at Southern Technical Institute, Marietta, Georgia. Since his major teaching area is technical writing, he combines vocation and avocation in the more than 100 trade journal articles he has published. His book, Principles of Technical Writing, was published by Addison-Wesley.

## Evelyn P. Johnson

Evelyn Johnson is editor of the Sommerville, Tennessee weekly The Fayette Falcon and has sold freelance articles, short stories, poems and fillers to a variety of publications.

## Etna M. Kelley

Etna M. Kelley, a free-lance writer, has made a specialty of writing articles about business anniversaries—so much so that she compiles yearly lists of companies about to celebrate their anniversaries. Her 1972 List of Company Birthdays ($15) includes more than 1200 companies marking their 25th, 50th, 75th, 100th, etc. year in business.

## M. Mable Lunz

The author started her career writing handicraft for children as a hobby. She has had articles, children's teen-age and adult stories published in various magazines and church school papers.

## Patt Kirby McCauley

Patt Kirby McCauley has been operating her own advertising
and public relations business for 10 years. "Although I do have
a small office," she says, "I do most of my work at home so I
can keep track of my little army (six children). I began writing at age 8 when my parents bought me a gelatin duplicator for
my birthday, with which I published the neighborhood *Town
Crier*. After the fourth issue, a neighbor threatened my father
with a law suit for libel and that ended my publishing career."
A graduate of the University of California, Mrs. McCauley was
an advertising copywriter with the San Francisco *Chronicle*
and an advertising agency before her marriage. She has sold
magazine articles and newspaper features and is currently at
work on a book, *The Trouble With Big Families is Small Children.*

## M. C. McCrory

Mrs. McCrory is a Marshalltown, Iowa writer especially interested in the many new opportunities now open in the field of
children's theater. Dr. Wenstrom is professor of English at
Denver's Metropolitan State College and the author of a number of entertainments produced for children.

## Ross R. Olney

Ross R. Olney has been a freelance writer for 18 years. His stories and articles have been published in many magazines and he
has published 14 other nonfiction books besides the one described in his article.

## Betty Stilwell Owens

"I have been entering contests as a hobby for about 16 years"
comments Betty Owens "and so far I've won almost $15,000
and innumerable appliances, sports equipment and other items.
Contesting adds excitement to your life, and lots of little and
big bonuses while you're making the long, hard pull of becoming a writer."

## Eugene Perrett

Since writing the chapter in this book, the author went on to become a staff writer with Phyllis Diller, then the Jim Nabors Hour. He is now in his second season with that show and also writes material for Bob Hope.

## Emalene Shepherd

The author has been a freelance writer since she was a teenager and has sold hundreds of articles to publications such as those described in her article. Her book, "The Student Journalist and Freelance Writing," was published by Richards Rosen Press.

## Jean Conder Soule

*Jean Conder Soule's* light verses have appeared in a variety of nationally-known magazines and newspapers including *The Wall Street Journal, Saturday Evening Post, Ladies' Home Journal, Better Homes and Gardens,* and *The Christian Science Monitor.* Mrs. Soule has also been the leader of juvenile writing and light verse workshops at the Philadelphia Regional Writers Conference.

## Irene Sullivan

Irene Sullivan was State Editor for the Lexington, Ky. Herald-Leader, at the time this article was written, and in that position provided much helpful guidance for her newspaper's correspondents with helpful newsletters on manuscript preparation, style, etc.

## Kirk Polking

Kirk Polking came to the Editorship of Writer's Digest after freelancing as a full-time writer for five years. Prior to this, she had been an Editorial Assistant on Writer's Digest and Modern Photography and Circulation Manager of The Farm Quarterly. Her published works include over 100 magazine articles and four books, the latest of which, *Let's Go to an Atomic Energy Town* (for children), was published by G. P. Putnam's Sons, in 1968. She has lectured on writing at numerous colleges and writers' workshops throughout the country.

# Index